What on Earth is the Church For?

What on Earth is the Church For?

A blueprint for the future for
Church based mission and social action

David Devenish

Authentic

12 11 10 09 08 07 06   8 7 6 5 4 3 2

First published 2005 by Authentic Media,
9 Holdom Avenue, Bletchley, Milton Keynes, Bucks, MK1 1QR, UK
and 129 Mobilization Drive, Waynesboro, GA 30830-4575, USA
www.authenticmedia.co.uk
Authentic Media is a division of Send the Light Ltd., a company limited by
guarantee (registered charity no. 270162)

British Library Cataloguing in Publication Data
A catalogue record for this book is available from the British Library

ISBN-13 978-1-86024-537-4

ISBN-10 1-86024-537-4

Cover design by four-nine-zero design.
Print Management by Adare Carwin
Printed in Great Britain by Haynes, Sparkford, Yeovil, Somerset

Contents

Contents

Acknowledgements

I want to thank Stephanie Hedley for typing up all the earlier drafts of this book from my dictation, and my secretary, Rebecca Woodward, for her subsequent hard work in working through the many amended versions. I am also grateful to Jane Sanders for her very helpful comments on the manuscript. Malcolm Down of Authentic Media originally encouraged me to write another book and has been very supportive and understanding through the delays in completing it. Once again my father, Roy Devenish, put together the Bible references in each chapter.

Chapter One

Introduction:
The Church Has a Great Future!

There is much debate today about the role and purpose of the church. How we contribute to this debate, however, depends on our perspective and experience. In the UK, we are regularly confronted with statistics about the decline of the church. It is my practice to listen to the debates on BBC Radio 4's *Today* programme while I shower in the mornings. Quite often fresh statistics are quoted, which claim to show the serious decline of church attendance and religious belief in England. And it is not only in the secular media that such despondency is expressed. I recently attended a Christian missions' conference where one speaker suggested that the situation regarding the decline of the UK church was so dire that we should seriously consider whether there would be an effective church at all in twenty or thirty years' time. He concluded that the contribution of the UK church to global mission in the future could well be non-existent.

In contrast to this, however, I see thousands of young people gathering during the summer to events such as 'Soul Survivor', 'Soul in the City' and 'Festival

Manchester', evidently enjoying God and wanting to make significant contributions to social conditions in our cities. In the family of churches to which I belong, we have just initiated a similar youth event where we witnessed 3,000 young enthusiasts sharing the gospel. I know the young people represented in these events are nationally a small minority, but they do offer a more encouraging perspective on the future of the church.

Across the World

In contrast to its apparent decline in our own nation, the church is growing phenomenally fast in parts of the developing world. As I travel there, the questions are not so much 'Is the church going to die out?' as 'How can we train enough leaders?', 'How can we ensure that our people are well discipled?', 'How can we, in our poverty, be involved in world mission, so that those who have not yet heard the gospel can do so?' Philip Jenkins comments, 'Christianity should enjoy a worldwide boom in the new century, but the vast majority of believers will be neither white, nor European, nor Euro-American.'[1]

Not many years ago, Christian interest in the church in the Soviet Union was focused on how we might help believers undergoing persecution. There were rallying cries, for example, concerning justice for the 'Siberian Seven', a group of persecuted Pentecostal believers who had sought refuge in the US Embassy in Moscow.[2] Yet when I travelled to Siberia recently, I was asked to speak on the subject of 'The Church and Mission' and was asked questions about how we can equip Siberian believers to reach the Islamic world with the gospel – a very different scenario from the beleaguered 'Siberian Seven'!

My purpose in writing this book is to argue that the whole purpose of the church on earth is *mission*. The church exists to be the agent of the kingdom of God, the agent of God's rule on earth, and the means of taking the gospel of that kingdom to every people group. I believe the church is very much at the centre of God's purposes, and it is my aim to present a high view of the church, not as a static pastoral community but as a vibrant, active body totally committed to world mission. What on earth is the church for? It exists for mission.

My Own Journey

In my own spiritual journey, I gained a new understanding of the *nature* of the church before I gained a clearer revelation of its *purpose*. Many of us in the west have an individualistic view of the Christian life, with the emphasis on 'personal salvation', a 'personal walk with God', a 'personal call' to a 'personal destiny' or 'personal ministry'. This bias towards the individual is the product of an Enlightenment world view and a western mind-set, and does not tend towards a high view of the church as the corporate people of God. For me, this individualistic view of the *nature* of Christianity changed radically, more than twenty years ago. But only more recently have I come to understand the *purpose* of the church in the context of witness, mission and bringing in the kingdom of God with its biblical emphasis on social justice and the relief of poverty.

The events leading up to my change of perspective are still very vivid in my memory. It was July 1981 and Scilla and I were going with our young children to our very first 'Bible Week'. We had heard of the Bible Week phenomenon and had been impressed by the effect on some young people we knew but we were very nervous about going. Bible Weeks were one of the expressions of the Charismatic Renewal Movement which had had an extraordinary impact on the church in Britain in the 1970s and 80s. People from all denominations and Christian backgrounds had discovered a fresh outpouring of the Holy Spirit and were gathering together for celebrations, weekend events, concerts such as the 'Come Together' events and for Bible Weeks with new forms of worship and prophetic teaching in an atmosphere of fun and relaxation for the whole family. I had just started to accept that all the gifts of the Holy Spirit were for today and our church was beginning to experience them, but the idea of thousands of people gathering for worship still filled us with trepidation. However, an enthusiast in our church had persuaded us and a few other families to book into the Dales Bible Week in Harrogate.

On the Sunday before the Bible Week, I received a phone call to the effect that I had to be in Nigeria the next day. At that time I was working as an international banker, negotiating project finance deals in developing countries. At stake were contracts worth many millions of pounds. This phone call was completely unexpected, but I made the arrangements that afternoon nevertheless, and was on a plane the next day. There followed a terrible week. I was ill the first night in Nigeria, after eating very suspect food; in the ramshackle hotel, local prostitutes kept banging on my door all through the night; I had to travel to different cities, sleeping in a different bed each night and did not know whether I would make it back in time for the Bible Week. In fact, I returned home on the Friday evening, totally exhausted, just in time to start packing the trailer for our major family expedition. We had never camped before, so I had no past experience to help me. When I could not get the rear lights on the trailer to work, it was the last straw. I completely lost my cool and regretted ever agreeing to go. By this time, I think my wife and children were regretting it, too!

The next day, however, we struggled up to Harrogate,

put up our tent for the first time and went to the evening meeting. We sat at the back, not really knowing what to expect. Others around us evidently enjoyed the worship, and then we sat down to listen to a man I had heard of but never met – Bryn Jones.

It was amazing. I cannot recall any particular sentence of his message but I was gripped by a vision I had never seen before. God spoke right into my heart, and revealed to me the truth and vision that have guided my life and ministry ever since: that God has a plan for a glorious end-time church – a church which expresses the life of God as a community and demonstrates the kingdom or rule of God as a 'city set on a hill' in every nation, city and village. I was introduced to the doctrine that was called at the time 'Restoration of the church'.

Restoration of the Church

Understanding this doctrine of restoration meant a complete change in my thinking. Scilla and I had been brought up in the Exclusive Brethren, where we had been taught a very different doctrine. The Exclusive Brethren were a small, strict group of Christians who, by the time we left, had effectively become a sect. Though they are few in number and not seen as important on the Christian scene today, some of the doctrines of John Nelson Darby, the founder of the group early in the nineteenth century, have had a massive effect on Christian thinking. One piece of teaching which has had wide influence is the doctrine of 'Dispensationalism', which is the belief that all history is divided into seven 'dispensations', or periods of time, in which God dealt in different ways with his people, and during which there were different means of salvation. The Exclusive Brethren further taught that each dispensation 'failed' shortly after its inception and that the church era was only a

parenthesis – a sort of diversion from God's main purpose – which occurred because the Jews of Jesus' day did
not receive the kingdom. At that point in the first century
AD, we were told, the 'prophetic clock' of God's unfolding purpose on earth stopped, and the church era or
'dispensation' started – and fell into ignominious failure
within thirty years of Pentecost, never to be fully
restored. The church would thereafter become increasingly small until rescued by Jesus at 'the rapture'.
Contrary to most teaching on the second coming up until
that time, Darby taught that there would be a 'secret'
rapture of the church, followed by a period of intense
suffering, after which Jesus would return publicly.

As I listened to Bryn Jones preach, God initiated a
complete revolution in my thinking and gave me a new
vision of the church. Before fully accepting this new
understanding, however, I needed to be confident that it
was in fact what the Bible taught. I started looking at the
prophetic scriptures with new eyes. I read books such as
The Puritan Hope by Ian Murray (The Banner of Truth
Trust, 1971), which showed that current pessimism about
the future of the church was the total opposite of the hope
that had inspired the Christians who revived evangelical
truth from the Reformation onwards. This 'hope' in turn
had influenced the missionary movement of the late
eighteenth century. All these men and women of God
believed in a glorious worldwide church yet to come, not
an ever-decreasing 'remnant'.

The Prophetic Hope
As I started to look again at the Old Testament
'Restoration prophecies' of a 'glorious Zion' that would
follow the captivity in Babylon, I found that the prophets
of that time spoke of a wonderful day to come when
Jerusalem would again be the praise of the whole earth.[3]

Other prophecies spoke of the mountain of the Lord being raised higher than the other mountains,[4] and of a kingdom with small beginnings becoming a mountain that fills the earth.[5] I began to see that the full extent of these glorious prophecies was not fulfilled by the return of a small minority of the Jewish people from captivity in Babylon to the land of Israel. Steven Travis described this return from captivity as 'more like the trickle homewards of the supporters of a fourth division football team after defeat in the first round of the cup, than like the thrill of a return of a jubilant cup winning team to their home town'.[6]

Then I saw that the New Testament writers applied these Restoration scriptures to what God was going to do through his church in blessing many nations. For example, Isaiah's prophecy, 'It is too small a thing for you to be my servant to restore the tribes of Jacob . . . I will also make you a light for the Gentiles, that you may bring my salvation to the ends of the earth'[7] is applied by Paul to the spread of the gospel to incorporate the nations [or Gentiles] into the people of God.[8]

Again, at the Council of Jerusalem in Acts 15, when the leaders of the church were debating the question of Gentiles receiving the gospel, they settled it with a quotation from another prophetic scripture,[9] this time Amos: 'After this I will return and rebuild David's fallen tent. Its ruins I will rebuild, and I will restore it, that the remnant of men may seek the Lord, and all the Gentiles who bear my name'.[10] This would appear at first sight to be a reference to the rebuilding of physical Jerusalem; the apostle James, however, applied it to the bringing of the nations into the people of God, i.e. the inclusion in the church of those from every nation.

I realised that it was important for us to interpret the Old Testament as the New Testament does – a sound hermeneutical principle. An even more conclusive example of this principle is provided by Paul in the letter to Galatians.[11] He quotes Isaiah 54:1 which clearly speaks of the future glory of Zion and applies it to the new covenant people of God, 'Sing, O barren woman, you who never bore a child; burst into song, shout for joy, you who were never in labour; because more are the children of the desolate woman than of her who has a husband.' The apostles interpreted Old Testament scriptures as relevant to the church and its mission in the New Testament era, rather than applying only to the Jews in the period of history in which they were first recorded. So we, too, should be confident in following their example and applying these Old Testament scriptures to the church in the same way.

A City on a Hill

One of the greatest Old Testament chapters concerning the blessing of the nations is Isaiah 60. It reads in terms of all the nations of the earth gathering to Zion, to the physical city of Jerusalem. However, if we interpret this prophecy according to the pattern given in the New Testament, we see it as looking forward to a time when God will gather people from every nation into the heavenly Jerusalem – the community of the redeemed. As Alec Motyer puts it in his commentary on that chapter, 'The gathering of the world into the embrace of the people of God is naturally seen in pilgrimage and tribute motifs. The reality is the winning of the nations by the gospel and the gathering of all into the heavenly Zion when the Lord Jesus returns.'[12]

And just as the prophets spoke of a gloriously restored 'city of God', so Jesus made a promise to his humble Galilean peasant followers: 'You are the light of the world. A city on a hill cannot be hidden.'[13] If this city is to be 'the praise of the [whole] earth' and every people group blessed by the gospel of the kingdom, then we must believe for the church to be indeed a 'city set on a hill' in every people group. This is what is meant by the 'Restoration of the church'. God has made promises: our vision for our local churches and for our own personal lives is to be full of hope in the light of these glorious 'Restoration' promises.

Restoration – Two Components

When this 'Restoration' understanding came alive again to the church in the UK, there were actually two important components to it. We must be careful not to confuse them or forget either of them. Firstly, what was meant by 'Restoration' was that the church should be restored to New Testament truth and New Testament practices. In terms of this first component, there has been a gradual 'Restoration' through the centuries. At the time of the Reformation, under the leadership of Martin Luther and others, there was a 'Restoration' of the truths that our salvation is by faith, and that Scripture alone is to be our authority for both doctrine and practice. Amongst the Anabaptists and 'Dissenters' in English church history, there was a recognition that the church should be free from the political control of the state. It was this freedom that many of the early American settlers sought to maintain. In the Brethren movement in the early nineteenth century, the practical understanding of the 'priesthood' of all believers was restored so that contributions to church services were expected from any believer. Then the Pentecostal outpouring at the beginning of the last century saw the 'Restoration' of the gifts of the Holy Spirit to the church. This was broadened through the charismatic movement which brought the understanding of the baptism of the Holy Spirit and spiritual gifts to many mainline denominations in the later part of the twentieth century. I am committed to this 'Restoration' of New Testament doctrine and practice to the church.

'Restoration', however, means more than this. There is a second component. As well as biblical doctrine and practice being restored (and we may still have much to learn in these areas), it means that *we put our hope in the prophetic promises of an end-time glorious church affecting every people group.* This is not 'triumphalistic' (i.e. taking an over-optimistic view which does not accord with reality). Sometimes people ask me, 'Do you think things will get better or worse before the second coming?' My answer is 'Both'. I believe that there will be a glorious church, but that it will be surrounded by an increase of evil. The spirit of antichrist is at work in this world,[14] and there will be trouble and conflict;[15] it is through difficulties that we enter the kingdom.[16] The church in parts of China today illustrates this apparent contradiction. Chinese Christians have experienced unprecedented revival but also widespread persecution, imprisonment and faithful endurance.

A Glorious Church

It was the expectation of Jesus himself that his kingdom would grow. He said it was like a mustard seed that would grow into a large tree, and like yeast which is added to bread in a small quantity, yet permeates the whole dough.[17]

It is because of my understanding of this doctrine of the glorious church and the growing kingdom of God on earth, that I am so committed to a positive outlook on the church today. I have noticed recently in the UK a growing disillusionment and sometimes cynicism about the church, as some Christians focus instead on living out the gospel 'in the world'. I am very supportive of the emphasis today on the importance of Christians working for the kingdom not only 'in church', but wherever we are, in our secular jobs, amongst our neighbours, in 'kingdom' social action projects. However, that right emphasis should not cause us to be cynical about the church or fail to recognise the importance of the local church. It has always been God's heart to have a people, a body, a bride for his Son. We are to be a corporate demonstration and witness to the world of God's power and love. God's heart is for community: a people for the Father, a bride for the Son, a temple to be a dwelling place of the Holy Spirit.

In Bedford . . .

The church is more important than my personal ministry. I remember vividly when Scilla and I became convinced that it was God's call for me to give up my secular job in international banking. As we prayed about it, it was not the prospect of major ministry that God used to call me, but the fact that a small church in the north-east corner of Bedford needed a leader. I was called to serve one local church, but with a vision of the prophetic purpose of God for his whole church worldwide.

In Russia . . .

I love to share this vision. About three years ago, I was speaking at a conference in Armavir in the North Caucasus region of Southern Russia. As I was about to speak, I felt God prompt me to discard my prepared message and speak from my heart (and without notes!) on God's glorious end time church. When I had finished, one of the older leaders present, Anatole Nicolayovich Bondorenko from Ukraine, said that this was the same truth which he had heard as a young man in communist times. During the 1950s, he had been discipled by a man imprisoned for his faith who, on his release, had taught about the glorious end-time church, based on exactly the same scriptures I had used that afternoon. Under the shadow of a communist system which seemed immensely powerful and never likely to fall, most of the Russian churches to whom he preached rejected his message, saying the church would just be a faithful remnant until the second coming. But as with every other empire throughout history, Soviet communism has fallen. The truth of 'Restoration' was preached in Russia in the 1950s; the same vision came into the charismatic movement in the 1970s; in earlier centuries, the same truth inspired many of the Puritans in England and energised the early missionary movement.

Away with Cynicism

It is a hope to be proclaimed today and held onto in resolute faith as we face up to the challenge of praying for world mission and sending people, until we see a glorious church in every people group. This vision will similarly sustain us in local church life as we encounter difficulties in relationships and other problems that come when imperfect people are gathered into community. Our pains and disappointments will be seen in the end, as the apostle Paul said, to be 'light and momentary troubles';[18] the seemingly powerful kingdoms of the world will, in the end, become 'the kingdom of our [God] and of his Christ';[19] the cause of Jesus Christ will triumph.

The great nineteenth-century preacher, C.H. Spurgeon, made this comment on Psalm 86:9 ('All the nations you have made will come and worship before you, O Lord; they will bring glory to your name'). The psalmist:

Was not a believer in the theory that the world would grow worse and worse, and the dispensation wind up with general darkness and idolatry. Earth's sun is to go down amid tenfold night if some of our prophetic brethren [Such as those who were promoting the view that I was brought up in!] are to be believed. Not so do we expect, but we look for a day when the dwellers in all lands shall learn righteousness, shall trust in the Saviour, shall worship Thee alone, O God, and shall glorify Thy Name. The modern notion has greatly dampened the zeal of the church for missions and the sooner it is shown to be unscriptural the better for the cause of God. It neither consorts with prophecy, honours God, nor inspires the church with ardour. Far hence be it driven.[20]

Amen to that! Far hence be driven cynicism about the future of the worldwide church or disillusionment with our local church! Instead, we need an assurance of faith based on the promises of God.

The Rule of God

I am thus totally committed to the doctrine of the church. But I am also totally committed to the doctrine of the kingdom. As I continued to study the word of God and in particular the 'Restoration' scriptures from the Old Testament prophets, I became aware that they were not only laying emphasis on the *people* of God, the new Zion. They were also speaking about the *rule* of God being manifested. They prophesied an age of justice instead of injustice, of 'good news to the poor', of the poor not only being reached for the gospel but the poor themselves becoming '. . . oaks of righteousness, a planting of the LORD for the display of his splendour'.[21]

This is of course consistent with what Jesus actually did. He came and preached the good news of the *kingdom*, the rule of God coming here on earth. It is the gospel of the *kingdom* that we preach in every people group. Surely, therefore, we should be equally concerned about this kingdom aspect of the church's mission.

In All of Life

Before I was in full-time ministry, I worked first as a civil servant, involved in international trade negotiations, and then as an international banker. This work had made me realise a number of things, including the following:

- As a civil servant, I was involved in a number of international negotiations; in particular, for a while I served on the first UN working party on the debt problems of developing countries. Obviously I was committed to reflecting government policy, but felt imprisoned within a policy which, at that time, failed either to recognise fully the depth of the problem of the indebtedness, or to give hope of a way through, which did not merely serve short-term economic interests. As I studied further the problem of poverty, I realised that in God's economy the issue of debt was dealt with through the radical Old Testament principle of Jubilee. 'At the end of every seven years you must cancel debts. This is how it is to be done . . .'[22] 'In this Year of Jubilee everyone is to return to his own property. If you sell land to one of your countrymen or buy any from him, do not take advantage of each other. You are to buy from your countryman on the basis of the number of years since the Jubilee. . . . what he sold will remain in the possession of the buyer until the Year of Jubilee. It will be returned in the Jubilee, and he can then go back to his property.'[23] Obviously, I could not apply these principles directly into the context of my work, but if the Christian message is about the rule or kingdom of God, then Christians should have something to say on these subjects which expresses the way in which that rule of God is to be exercised.

- I also realised that in much of its preaching, the church did not really address many of the problems I was facing at work. Much of our teaching touches on issues of personal salvation and life within the church. Understanding the kingdom of God is far broader than this. It affects how I function as a Christian in the market-place; it affects my political perspectives; it affects how I handle my staff. Even unbelievers realise this. I was once in the former Yugoslavia, chatting late into the night with some business colleagues. We started talking about Christianity, and one of the men said that he believed in the Christian message because his wife had been miraculously healed in a charismatic Christian meeting, having been crippled for many years, but that he himself could not become a Christian. I inquired why. He said it would mean him giving up his job, because he was there in Yugoslavia selling something that people did not really need; it was not in their best interest to buy his product. So how could he continue to sell his product, with integrity, if he became a Christian!

When I came into full-time Christian ministry leading a church, I began to try and bring these things together. As a church is returned to the biblical pattern, it will be a church that reaches the poor and needy and dispossessed, those without a voice. Consequently, when I was praying about the future and seeking to develop the vision for our church, I remember writing down that in the next five years we would see a house established which would care effectively for the homeless in our town. When I was first invited to speak from the main platform at a Bible Week (something I never dreamt I would do when I attended my first Bible Week!) I preached on the subject of Daniel, as an example of some-body who brought in the kingdom of God whilst remain-ing in full-time secular work. I wanted to bring a sense of dignity to those who have a passion for the kingdom of God and want to see that worked out in a secular environment.

Church and Kingdom

The social action or kingdom aspects of the gospel need to be restored to the church as well as the aspects of New Testament doctrine and practice, if the church is to be fully restored to the biblical promises. My concern is that those with a kingdom emphasis often function separately from the local church, though local churches may be asked to support them. But a high view of both church and kingdom will lead us to see both social action and mission as the clear responsibility of the local church. Indeed, that is what the church is here on earth for. My own theological journey has led me to a vision of a glorious church, devoted to Jesus, devoted to truth, devoted to one another – but also devoted to mission and committed to kingdom social action.

Notes

1 Philip Jenkins, *The Next Christendom* (Oxford University Press, 2002), p. 2
2 Story told in Danny Smith, *Who Says You Can't Change the World?* (Spring Harvest Publishing/Authentic, 2003)
3 Isaiah 62:7
4 Isaiah 2:2
5 Daniel 2:35
6 Steven Travis, *I Believe in the Second Coming of Jesus* (Hodder & Stoughton, 1982), p.126
7 Isaiah 49:6
8 Acts 13:47

9 Amos 9:11,12
10 Acts 15:16,17
11 See Galatians 4:27
12 Alec Motyer, *The Prophecy of Isaiah* (IVP, 1993), p. 495
13 Matthew 5:14
14 1 John 4:3
15 John 16:33
16 Acts 14:22
17 Matthew 13:31–33
18 2 Corinthians 4:17
19 Revelation 11:15
20 C.H. Spurgeon, *The Treasury of David Volume II* (MacDonald Edition), p. 466
21 Isaiah 61:3
22 Deuteronomy 15:1,2
23 Leviticus 25:13–15,28

Chapter Two

What Then is the Purpose of the Church?

'How did you come to know Jesus?' I asked the young man who was sitting in front of me. Scilla and I were hosting a conference for pastors and wives in Southern Russia, and one mealtime we had been introduced to a man from one of the many minority Islamic people groups in the Caucasus mountains. Few from these people groups have come to Christ, so we were very interested in how this man had been converted from Islam. He told us that he had previously been a gangster and had got into a fight and been sent to prison, where he gradually became so depressed that he decided to take his own life. He turned his hands towards us and showed us deep scars on his wrists. After cutting his wrists he passed out, but as he lay in a coma, a man appeared to him and said, 'Follow me.' My friend inquired, 'Are you Mohammed?' 'No, I am Jesus,' the man replied, and then showed my friend a vision of hell and said again, 'Will you follow me?' My friend said, 'Yes, I will follow you.' At that moment, he came out of his coma healed, both of his wounds and his despair. He then committed his life to following Jesus, both in prison and when he got out.

There are many stories like this one, from the Islamic world in particular. Again and again, it seems that people who have not yet heard or believed the gospel – some of them seeking after God, some of them in despair – are receiving visions of Jesus, or appearances of angels. This is a sovereign work of God, and to me it illustrates his great passion to reach into all the people groups of the world, even before the missionaries can get there! It is a moving experience to catch such a glimpse of what is on God's heart. But of course, his passion to reach out to the nations is nothing new, and was built into the very heart of the purpose of the church from its beginning, by Jesus himself.

The Essence of the Church

I believe that John's gospel offers us particular insights into what was on the heart of Jesus as he started the church. Almost half of its twenty-one chapters describe the final week of Jesus' life: his conversations with his disciples in the Upper Room, his trial and crucifixion and, of course, his resurrection. It is therefore in this gospel that we have some of the most intimate insights into what was on his mind at the very crux of his mission on earth, immediately before and after he died. If we want to understand what Jesus was passionate about, I believe we could look in no better places than his last recorded prayer shortly before his arrest, and his first conversation with the embryonic church after his resurrection.

Jesus' prayer in John 17 contains both the personal concerns he brought before his Father, and also his priorities for his followers. Even as he contemplates his own final suffering, Jesus prays for the church he has formed during his ministry and the leaders he has trained, and he looks forward through time and prays for the church throughout history, for all those who will believe through the message of his apostles. Then in John

20, Jesus speaks to his followers at the very first meeting of the embryonic church after the momentous events of the crucifixion and resurrection.[1]

There is one key statement that Jesus makes on both these occasions. The fact that he repeated it at these two key moments demonstrates, I believe, its importance as the essence, the purpose, the very DNA of the church. On the first occasion, speaking to his Father, Jesus says, 'As you [Father] sent me into the world, I have sent them into the world'.[2] On the second occasion, he says to his astonished and fearful disciples after the resurrection, 'As the Father has sent me, I am sending you'.[3] It seems that Jesus regards his church as a people who are called together for the very purpose of being sent into the world – in other words, he calls us for mission!

A Sent Community

As we saw in Chapter One, it is important to see the church restored to its New Testament pattern. We want the church to be everything it was intended to be. Very often in teaching about ecclesiology (the technical term for the 'doctrine of the church'), the emphasis is on the church being a people called out from the world. Whilst this is true, it is only a part of the truth. The purpose of God in calling us together is *to send us into the world with a mission*. The essence of the church is 'missional'. The idea of 'being sent' is not a secondary addition or an optional extra.

Evangelical Christians often talk about 'doing evangelism'. 'Does your church do any evangelism?' 'What evangelism does your church do?' But according to these statements of Jesus, the whole point of the church's existence is mission or evangelism! In many churches there is a small group of enthusiasts who are 'concerned about mission'. They meet together regularly to pray for those who have been sent to other nations with the gospel, and keep in touch with them. This is good and I am sure that many in other nations have seen it as a lifeline. However, in practice it can promote the wrong idea that 'mission' is a separate and subsidiary department of the church's work unless the overall prayer focus of the church is geared towards its mission. All the major Christian denominations have a 'missions department', and people who sense the calling of God to go elsewhere with the gospel will consider 'What organisation should we join, since we want to be involved in mission?' If we understand the essentially missional nature of the church, however, this 'missionary society' way of looking at things may be seen to be a contradiction in terms. The whole essence of the church is that it exists for mission. We already belong to a mission agency – that's what the church is! That's the very reason why the church is here in the world!

The Earth Will Be Filled

We will return later to our consideration of Jesus' words in John 17 and 20, but first it is important that we understand that they are not isolated statements, but fully in line with God's purpose throughout Scripture. God has a plan to fill the earth with his glory.[4] This is spoken of prophetically and celebrated in song several times in the Old Testament. What does it mean, to fill the earth with God's glory? In one sense the whole of creation, despite being marred as a result of humanity's sin, reveals the glory of God in its intricacy and beauty, for those who have eyes to see it. I believe, however, that it means more than this. It certainly does not mean that the whole earth will be filled with a warm, fuzzy, golden light as in our Sunday school imagination of glory! Rather, it means that all over the world, there will be multitudes of people living for the praise of God's glory. Jesus told us that the Father is seeking worshippers, worshippers who are no longer concerned with so-called 'holy places' in which to worship God, whether a mountain in Samaria or a temple in Jerusalem, but who will worship the Father in spirit and in truth wherever they are, in every city, town and village;[5] people who are worshippers of God and who seek to live their lives to his glory.

The command to Adam and Eve, the pinnacle of God's creation, made in his image, was from the very outset to 'fill the earth'.[6] It was a call to fill it not only with their children, but with the rule of God. The idea of 'ruling' was an essential element of being created in the image of God. Genesis 2 shows man almost as an estate manager. Right from the beginning, humanity's role was not to dominate or exploit but to exercise responsible steward-ship which recognises that all things derive their exis-tence from God's hand.[7]

The purpose was to fill the earth with people who reflect God, praise God, live for the glory of God and establish the rule or kingdom of God.

However, Adam and Eve sinned and God's original purpose to fill the earth with his glory was not fulfilled; the earth was certainly filled, but with men and women who sought to emulate Adam and Eve and be as gods ('like God'),[8] autonomous beings, claiming to be in charge of their own destiny. As people spread out across the earth after the flood, their objective was to make a name for themselves, to reach the heavens,[9] to achieve personal autonomy and fulfilment instead of the glory of God. That is still what humanity without Christ is seeking to do.

Every Clan

After God had brought judgement on that sinful ambition by confusing the languages at the Tower of Babel, he again made a promise about filling the earth and blessing every people group, when he called Abraham and said to him, '. . . all peoples on earth will be blessed through you'.[10] This promise was later clarified as, 'Through your offspring all nations on earth will be blessed, because you have obeyed me'.[11] As each nation receives the blessing of God through the descendants of Abraham, so the earth will be filled with his glory. Indeed, as Dewi Hughes points out, 'all peoples' is literally 'all families'. 'The term used here could be translated "clan" – a collective unit that is bigger than a father's household but smaller than a tribe.'[12] Every clan is to be blessed through the seed of Abraham, so that the glory of God will increasingly fill the earth.

When Jesus had risen from the dead, he called his disciples to him and gave them instructions which echoed the original command to Adam and Eve: Fill the earth with disciples.[13] In every nation let there be those who live for the glory of God as they obey the commands of Christ. God's intention is still to fill the earth with his glory and we are privileged to be part of that.

True Holiness

The two key passages I highlighted in John's gospel are consistent with this intention. They are the two key chapters in which Jesus says what the church is actually to be like – his prayer for the church, and the first ever church meeting! In John 17, Jesus prays, 'Sanctify them by the truth; your word is truth. As you have sent me into the world, I have sent them into the world. For them I sanctify myself, that they too may be truly sanctified.'[14] It is clear that the context of our sanctification is our being sent into the world. True sanctification or holiness means to be set apart for God's mission to the world. The word 'sanctified' literally means to be 'set apart' exclusively for God's purpose, 'set apart' for sacred duty. It was a familiar idea in the Old Testament. Jeremiah was 'sanctified' or 'set apart' to be a prophet.[15] Aaron and his sons were 'sanctified' or 'consecrated' (same word) to be priests.[16] Jesus was 'set apart' for his mission to come and die to save a people. That people, the church, are in turn 'set apart' to God for their mission to go into the world as Jesus did. As D.A. Carson puts it, 'In John's gospel such sanctification is always for mission'.[17] This is true biblical holiness.

Those, like me, who have been brought up in a traditional and somewhat legalistic religious background will have heard many ideas of what true holiness is. It usually consisted of a long list of 'don'ts' and the occasional 'do'. Biblical holiness is not like this at all. The truth is that we please God as we walk free through his grace and in the power of the Holy Spirit. As we 'live by the Spirit', we will not 'gratify the desires of the sinful nature'.[18] In John 17, Jesus says, '[I am not praying] that you take them out of the world'.[19] This might seem an odd expression; when we pray we do not normally explain to God what we are not praying for! So why did Jesus say this? I believe it was included to help us understand an important truth.

Many Christians through the centuries have misinterpreted biblical holiness as 'being taken out of the world' – into a monastery or a Christian evangelical ghetto. Many would misunderstand holiness as 'having as little to do with the world as possible'. True holiness, however, is the opposite of withdrawal from the world; rather, it is being set apart by God for the very purpose of being sent into the world, to encounter the world, to mix with the world, in order to fill the world with disciples of Jesus. It is, in fact, the very thing that Jesus was accused of by the religious people of his day – going to parties, mixing with sinners, eating and drinking. It is in this context of going into the world that Jesus prays for us that we would be protected from the evil one.[20] It is precisely because the church is sent into the enemy's domain that we need such protection.

We find the urgency of Jesus concerning this same message after his resurrection. His first word when he appears to his disciples is 'Peace', or in Hebrew, 'Shalom'.[21] He says it twice for emphasis. No doubt this was to comfort his disciples who were full of fear in their locked room, but there is more to 'shalom' than comfort. It is a word that means not only a passive freedom from hostility and fear, but also wholeness, healing, forgiveness, reconciliation, fellowship, blessing and prosperity. I believe that Jesus means 'shalom' to be characteristic of the church in the world.

Sent as Jesus was Sent

And in no time at all, having established the 'shalom' character of his community, Jesus introduces the purpose of the community. Imagine the reaction of the disciples. They already knew what it meant to be sent into the world as Jesus had been sent! They had seen him enduring opposition, misunderstanding and eventually death, and they had also seen the positive aspects of being sent: demonstrating love for the unlovely and touching the untouchable. They would have understood the dynamic power of being sent – healing the sick, setting free the demonised, even raising the dead. This is what the church exists for!

There is the same urgency of Jesus in all the resurrection accounts. In Matthew it is the inevitable outworking of the risen Christ, who declares, 'All authority in heaven and on earth has been given to me'.[22] All the nations now belong to Jesus, so he tells his disciples to go and get them and make disciples of them. In Mark, Jesus rebukes the disciples for their lack of faith and then tells them: Go into all of creation.[23] It is in this context of being sent that the promise of signs and wonders following them to establish their message, is given.

Not 'Times and Dates'

In Luke's writings, the call to mission is specific and strategic. There is first a rebuke which the church still needs to heed today: please do not be preoccupied with times and dates concerning the second coming or the establishment of the kingdom.[24] We have a task to fulfil. We are to be concerned with mission, not the details of the times and dates. In the disciples' minds there was in any case a real misunderstanding about the kingdom. I suggest that often today, Christians may be more concerned with speculation about dates and events than with our purpose of mission – just like the disciples!

In *Time* magazine, Nancy Gibbs wrote about the massive interest in end-time teachings since the events of September 11. She points out that the *Left Behind* series is read 50 per cent by those who are not evangelical Christians. She then goes on to write that if Christians are called to put their trust in Christ, it undermines that trust to focus on what cannot be known rather than on what must be done, e.g. healing the sick, helping the poor and spreading the gospel.[25] Here is a secular writer telling Christians that the church's priority should be strategic mission! That is exactly what Jesus is saying in Acts. So let us begin at our Jerusalem, go to our Judea, encounter with love our Samaria and reach the ends of the earth.

Message of Peace

Events such as 9/11 should make us more determined to reach the Middle East with the good news about Jesus. Our focus is to be the victory of the gospel of peace, not a military victory. This was the whole point of how Jesus was first sent. People were expecting a military victory over the Romans, but Jesus came with a message of peace that turned these expectations upside down. This was one reason why he was misunderstood and rejected by many of his Jewish contemporaries, and I believe many Christians can likewise misunderstand this principle today. Rather than looking only for political or military solutions, we are looking for a change in people's hearts, as the good news of the message of the 'shalom' that comes through Jesus Christ reaches a world in conflict. This is part of what it means to be sent as Jesus was sent.

So how was Jesus sent? Of course in one sense, the sending of Jesus was unique. Only he could atone for our sins, 'and not only for ours but also for the sins of the whole world'.[26] However, I want to suggest four ways in which the church is sent into the world as Jesus was sent, and these will be amplified throughout this book.

Kingdom Perspective

Firstly, Jesus was sent to announce and bring the kingdom of God. This was his manifesto. Repent, turn right around, change your total outlook on life! This includes turning away from my personal sins in repentance, but it is more than that. It is a commitment to God's new programme to bring everything in heaven and earth under one Head – Christ. It is global, it is to turn upside down the kingdoms of this world. It is to implement the hopes of the prophets who prophesied this coming of the kingdom; bringing justice, in a world of injustice; bringing freedom to those so disadvantaged and crushed they can hardly lift up their heads; setting free those for whom life is a monotonous grind under cruel exploitation.

The kingdom, as we will see, is a much bigger concept than my personal salvation. It is a broader concept even than the church. The church is the agent to bring the kingdom of God into this world through a commitment to Jesus' manifesto. 'The Spirit of the Lord is on me, because he has anointed me to preach good news to the poor. He has sent me to proclaim freedom for the prisoners and recovery of sight for the blind, to release the oppressed, to proclaim the year of the Lord's favour.'[27] So being sent as Jesus was sent will mean a kingdom perspective. It will affect how we relate to the world, and what we bring to it:

- How we help the poor
- How we conduct ourselves in the world of work and business
- How we work for justice
- How we show compassion for street children and drug addicts
- How we see the oppressed set free.

Kingdom Community

Secondly, Jesus was sent to form a community, the church. John 17 is a church planter's prayer, and to see it in this light makes sense of the prayer: 'Father protect this church'. Jesus was not praying for the world at this point, he was praying for the church. Father give them joy;[28] set them apart for the purpose of mission; let them be united; and let those who are reached through their apostolic mission similarly be protected and united. Jesus' purpose was to form a community that would reach the world, and welcome those saved out of the world into that community. In Acts 2, when the gospel was first preached, there was already a community of believers to which people could be added. '. . . three thousand were added to their number that day'.[29] '. . . more and more men and women believed in the Lord and were added to their number'.[30] In our evangelism we tend to count our success in terms of those who have made some sort of profession of faith, either by 'coming forward' or 'raising a hand' or showing interest in an Alpha course. While none of these are to be despised, we should note that in the New Testament, people were not counted as converts until they had become part of the church.

The Trinity
It is worth noting at this point that both mission and community have their origins in the doctrine of the Trinity. The Trinity of Father, Son and Holy Spirit, functioning in loving relational unity, is the perfect community. The Trinity is also the model of mission. The Father sends the Son; the Father and Son send the Holy Spirit. The Trinity is perfect community, and community in mission. So in the church, Jesus forms a community that reflects these qualities of the Trinity. He says, 'May they also be in us' – *community*, 'That the world may believe'[31] – *mission*. Similarly Jesus had said to the disciples earlier, 'Love one another' – *community*, 'By this all men will know' – *mission*.[32]

Kingdom Service
Thirdly, Jesus was sent to serve. The biblical word 'servant' is wonderfully rich in its meaning. It embraces both the dignity of the Anointed One ('chosen one'),[33] but is also the appropriate attitude for a Christian leader, who should genuinely regard himself as a 'slave' to people, rather than standing presumptuously on that

dignity. The idea of dignity attached to servanthood is something that cannot be understood outside of the example of Christ. However, being sent as Jesus was sent means that we take this attitude. In the book of Isaiah there is a collection of what are often called 'Servant Songs', in which the term 'servant' sometimes refers prophetically to Christ and sometimes to the people of God. We are now the corporate anointed servant, with the dignity of God's commissioning and the power of the Holy Spirit upon us. Our mission, like his, is to bring justice to the nations.

Incarnational

Because we have the dignity of being a servant, we can wash people's feet as Jesus did. Leaders in the Christian church have dignity as servants of God, so as Jesus[34] said, leaders do not need external titles like 'Rabbi', 'Father', 'Pastor' or 'Reverend'. Their dignity is to be found not in titles, but in an expression of a servanthood lifestyle and ministry. Our Christian servanthood is not only to the church but to the world as well, in what is often called 'incarnational mission'. Jesus came into human flesh in a particular culture at a particular time of much oppression, and served people. He touched lepers; he let prostitutes wash his feet; he constantly challenged attitudes and practices that excluded people. 'Jesus turns to all people who have been pushed aside: to the sick who are segregated on cultic and ritual grounds, to the prostitute and sinners who are ostracised on moral grounds, and to the tax collectors who are excluded on religious and political grounds. Tax collectors and prostitutes may even be praised by Jesus as models to emulate since they heed his call while others do not' – David Bosch.[35]

I am thrilled when I hear of situations where the world recognises that the church is serving people in need. One of the churches I work with is in Krasny Luch, Ukraine. Recently the town authorities asked the church there to provide care for difficult young people in the town. Praise God that in a once communist country, authorities are now turning to the church to meet needs in the community.

Cross-Cultural

Serving also means that we are prepared to get involved with other cultures. The gospel truths are unchanging, but we adapt as servants to each culture in order to reach each culture. 'Though I am free and belong to no man, I make myself a *slave* to everyone, to win as many as possible' (my emphasis).[36] We become like slaves to other cultures in order to reach people in that culture, including, as in the New Testament, different cultures in the same town, and in the same church.

Kingdom Mission

Fourthly, Jesus was sent to all the nations. At first sight, as we read the New Testament, this would not seem to be Jesus' mission. After all, he ministered mainly within Jewish territory. He seemed to put off a Gentile woman who wanted her daughter set free from a demon.[37] He told the disciples to concentrate on Jewish villages when he sent them out.[38] However, in Luke 4, when Jesus announced his kingdom manifesto, to which I have already referred, Luke records that, 'The eyes of everyone in the synagogue were fastened on him'.[39] I believe they were fascinated by him for several reasons:

- His authority very obviously attracted people to him.[40]
- The text he read was a favourite text of those waiting for the Messiah to come and overthrow the Roman yoke. They were waiting for the day of the Lord's

favour to come upon Israel.

- Jesus left out the 'best bit' of the reading so far as they were concerned; he did not include the words, 'the day of vengeance of our God',[41] which was how Isaiah had finished the sentence. They were expecting the restoration of Israel to be accompanied by judgement upon their enemies, in this case the Romans. Why had Jesus omitted 'the day of vengeance'? How could he announce one promise without the other?

Then Jesus confronted their limited view of God as the God of the Jews alone, and this enraged them. He said there were many widows in Israel in Elijah's time, yet they were not who the prophet was sent to. There were many in Israel with leprosy in the time of Elisha, yet it was not they but Naaman, a Syrian, who was healed.[42] In other words, Jesus was pointing out that the nations around Israel, enemy nations, had been blessed by the prophets Elijah and Elisha. I believe Jesus' audience got the message; I believe they understood why Jesus had not referred to vengeance upon the nations around Israel. They understood Jesus to be implying that while God's day of judgement will come, it is a future day, and until that time there is a gospel of peace to all the nations. God wants to fulfil his promise to Abraham and bless all the nations. This did not sit comfortably with their desire to see the supremacy of their own land and nation restored, and thus they became angry with Jesus and drove him from the synagogue.

Jesus did not share his contemporaries' concern for the integrity of the land of Israel; he was being sent on a much bigger mission. Though the land of Israel had functioned as an important focus of the life and faith of God's people in the Old Testament, the New Testament has a much wider perspective. 'The land no longer functioned as the key symbol of the geographical identity of the people of God, and that for obvious reasons: if the new community consisted of Jew, Greek, Barbarian alike, there was no sense in which one piece of territory could possess more significance than another. At no point in this early period do we find Christians eager to define or defend a "holy land". Jesus and the church together are the new temple; the world, I suggest, is the new land' (N.T. Wright).[43] Abraham was described by Paul as 'heir of the world'.[44] One land, one nation, is too small a focus for the purposes and promises of God. The prophets declared that it was too small a thing to restore the tribes of Israel.[45] The 'land' in the Old Testament was like a down payment of God's promises – the first instalment of the blessing of the whole world, every nation.

This, then, is why the church is in the world. It is here for mission, a mission to bring about the rule of God in the world, to start communities of God's people from all backgrounds in every people group, to serve the world through social action and in their everyday employment, and to extend this to every people group on earth. Evangelism and mission are not additional functions of the church in which only the most keen and enthusiastic members become involved. They are the whole raison d'être for the church's existence.

Let the Nations Be Glad

What on earth is the church for? It exists for mission. What is mission for? *Mission exists in order to bring glory to God.* Jesus came to establish the kingdom of God because the Father is seeking worshippers who will live their lives to bring glory to him. This must challenge every local church and its programmes: Do they fulfil the reason why we are here – to be sent into the world as Jesus was sent, in order for the earth to be filled with the knowledge of the glory of the Lord? Let the whole earth be filled with his glory. Let all the peoples praise him. As John Piper points out, 'Missions is not the ultimate goal of the church. Worship is. Missions exist because worship doesn't . . . The goal of missions is the gladness of the peoples in the greatness of God . . . "Let the peoples praise Thee, O God, Let all the peoples praise Thee! Let the nations be glad and sing for joy" (Psalm 67:3,4)'.[46]

Notes

1 John 20:19–23
2 John 17:18
3 John 20:21
4 Habakkuk 2:14; Psalm 72:19
5 John 4:23
6 Genesis 1:28
7 This is the inference drawn from the 'take care of it' in Genesis 2:15
8 Genesis 3:5
9 Genesis 11:4
10 Genesis 12:3
11 Genesis 22:18
12 Dewi Hughes, *Castrating Culture* (Paternoster Press, 2002), p. 75
13 Matthew 28:19
14 John 17:17–19
15 Jeremiah 1:5
16 Leviticus 8:30
17 D.A. Carson, *The Gospel According to John* (IVP, 1991), p. 566
18 Galatians 5:16
19 John 17:15
20 John 17:15
21 John 20:19
22 Matthew 28:18
23 Mark 16:15
24 Acts 1:7
25 Nancy Gibbs, *Time* magazine, 1 July 2002
26 1 John 2:2
27 Luke 4:18,19
28 John 17:13
29 Acts 2:41
30 Acts 5:14

31 See John 17:21–23
32 See John 13:34–35
33 See Isaiah 42:1
34 Matthew 23:7–10
35 David J. Bosch, *Transforming Mission* (Orbis, 1991), p. 27
36 1 Corinthians 9:19
37 Mark 7:25–27
38 Matthew 10:5,6
39 Luke 4:20
40 Matthew 7:29
41 Isaiah 61:2
42 Luke 4:25–27
43 N.T. Wright, *The New Testaments and People of God* (SPCK, 1992), p. 366
44 Romans 4:13
45 Isaiah 49:6
46 John Piper, *Let the Nations be Glad* (IVP, 1993), p. 11

Chapter Three

The Importance of Church Planting to Reach the Nations

Two or three years ago, Newfrontiers were considering, as a family of churches, sending a new church planting team to a particular country in the Middle East. I had a very helpful discussion over lunch with the Middle East Director of one of the mission agencies functioning in that region, following which we have been able to co-operate together in that particular country. One thing he said to me during that lunch made a great impact on me. He said that in that particular nation there were a number of isolated believers, many of whom had been converted as a result of radio ministry. A small proportion of these believers were being discipled individually, but there were no indigenous churches and he therefore welcomed our desire to plant churches.

As I came to understand much more about the situation, I found there had been a number of attempts to see small indigenous churches planted, but it had proved very difficult. Not only was there a real threat of persecution, but also indigenous believers were finding it very difficult to build trust with one another outside of family networks. Furthermore, there had been a great danger of new believers becoming dependent emotionally, spiritually and even financially upon expatriate missionaries. The result of this was that many Christian workers in that nation were engaged in other forms of Christian work, rather than church planting. Indeed, some had specifically excluded church planting from their mission objectives.

As I have travelled to other countries where church planting has been difficult, I have found similar situations. I know of one major city in a largely unreached nation where there are many Christian workers from all over the world involved in 'ministry' other than church planting, and yet there are not enough mature Christians to disciple and nurture new believers in the faith in the context of new churches. There are churches crying out for people to lead small groups and to train leaders, yet the Christian workers are too busy to do so. It seems strange that there are insufficient people to nurture new Christians in places where the population of Christian workers in 'full-time Christian ministry' equals or even exceeds the number of local believers. I recognise that many mission agencies do excellent work. Many have been pioneering gospel preaching and Christian literature distribution in difficult situations, sowing the seed so that others of us may reap. However, I am still bound to wonder whether, in our reluctance to plant churches, we have strayed from the priorities of apostolic mission in the New Testament.

More Than Conversion

Writing of the urgency to see people saved in Luke's account of the mission of Jesus and the early church, David Bosch comments, 'Personal conversion is not a goal in itself. To interpret the work of a church as the "winning of souls" is to make conversion into a final product, which flatly contradicts Luke's understanding of mission. Conversion does not pertain merely to an individual's act of conviction and commitment; it moves the individual believer into the community of believers and involves a real – even a radical – change in the life of the believer, which carries with it moral responsibilities that distinguish Christians from "outsiders", while at the same time stressing their obligation to those "outsiders".[1] In other words, the purpose of conversion is to lead us into God's new community, which is itself to be a light to the world.

Today, in missions training, one of the standard textbooks is Roland Allen's timeless volume *Missionary Methods – St Paul's or Ours?* Roland Allen was an Anglican missionary in North China working with the Society for the Propagation of the Gospel. His book, first published in 1912, remains a classic exposition of New Testament methods of mission and how they are to be applied in our time. Much less politely than I am doing in this chapter, he makes the same point in the introduction to his book: 'Men have wandered over the world, "preaching the Word", laying no solid foundations, establishing nothing permanent, leaving no really instructed society behind them, and have claimed St Paul's authority for their absurdities.'[2] He also comments that, 'Many missionaries in later days have received a larger number of converts than St Paul; many have preached over a wider area than he; but none have so established churches. We have long forgotten that such things could be. We have long accustomed ourselves to accept it as an axiom of missionary work that converts in a new country must be submitted to a very long probation and training, extending over generations, before they can be expected to stand alone.'[3]

Strong indigenous communities of God's people, who themselves reached many others with the gospel, were the product of Paul's missionary journeys, such as the church in Thessalonica of whom it is recorded, 'The Lord's message rang out from you not only in Macedonia and Achaia – your faith in God has become known everywhere.'[4] Church planting was Paul's priority, and church planting must be the missionary priority today. Both in our own home nation and in the unreached people groups of the world, more communities of God's people are needed if the prophetic purposes of God are to be fulfilled in the earth.

Church planting was very high on the agenda in debate amongst evangelicals in the UK a few years ago. The Dawn 2000 initiative was launched with a view to seeing many new churches planted, not only in unreached lands, but in countries like Britain, which has had the gospel for centuries, but which is now sorely in need of re-evangelisation. I think all agree on the urgency of this need but somehow, the impetus behind church planting has declined since the early 1990s. My prayer is for the renewal of the church such that even though many 'official' places of worship may close, new churches meeting in school halls, old church buildings, cinemas or factory units, may be multiplied across the land. This is absolutely indispensable for the re-evangelisation of our nation.

God Speaks to Us on Holiday!

A few years ago Scilla and I, with our two daughters, had a wonderful family holiday in Turkey. We enjoyed our times on the beach and in the sea but, like most tourists visiting that region, we also made a number of coach excursions to sights of historic interest. During one of these trips we visited Ephesus. It was an inspiring experience, walking through the ruins of the city where, despite it being a centre of occult practices in New Testament times, Paul had had probably his most successful church planting venture.

On another day we visited the warm springs of Pammukkale, close to the sites of the biblical cities of Colossae, Laodicea and Hierapolis, where churches were planted from Ephesus – almost certainly by those trained by Paul in his 'church planting school' in the hall of Tyrannus. We read how Paul trained the disciples daily in that lecture hall for two years, with the result that 'all the Jews and Greeks who lived in the province of Asia heard the word of the Lord'.[5] Colossae, Hierapolis and Laodicea were in that province, and evidently Epaphras had taken the gospel there.[6]

As we travelled back in the coach, I began to think how far it was from Ephesus to Pammukkale, especially at a time when travel was much slower than by coach! As I did so, I sensed the Holy Spirit come upon me in my seat and God started to speak to me. A whole region of churches was planted from Ephesus and so it was evidently possible to plant not just one church, but many churches in a region. I then felt God saying to me, 'Ask me for fifty churches in the Midlands area of England before the end of the year 2000.' So I started to pray that simple prayer, which I prayed many times over the next few months. Thus was launched what we in the Newfrontiers family of churches called 'The Midlands Initiative', a programme for planting new churches in the Midlands region. At the end of 2000 when I felt my commission there was completed, I handed over to a team led by David Stroud, whom I had trained for many years since he was seventeen years old. Not quite fifty churches in the Midlands area had been planted, but we were well on the way to that figure as a result of that initiative. I had previously overseen the planting of churches within my home town of Bedford, but my experience on the bus in Turkey gave me faith for a wider vision of church planting.

Why Plant Churches?

I would suggest the following important reasons why church planting is essential to a true missionary vision:

- **The Bride of Christ**
  Because it is a very high New Testament value. Not only is the universal church described as the bride of Christ, but so is the local church.[7] Paul has a wonderful way of moving from the huge, international, eschatological perspective of the church as the bride of Christ after Jesus' return, to his desire to see a particular local church, full of difficulties and problems, (as was the church in Corinth), being presented 'a pure virgin' to Christ. Similarly, the term the 'body of Christ' is used both of the universal church,[8] and of the local church.[9] To the New Testament apostles, it was not sufficient simply to evangelise; they were determined also to plant local churches, communities of God's people where the presence of God was experienced; communities who could corporately shine out in a dark world.[10]

- **Spiritual warfare**
  Because in the New Testament, the church was seen as the effective instrument of spiritual warfare. Jesus said, '. . . I will build my church, and the gates of Hades will not overcome it'.[11] It is through the church that the multicoloured wisdom of God is displayed to the principalities and powers,[12] the spiritual forces seen in Scripture as being behind what goes on in this world. Many talk about spiritual warfare today as if it was a

separate enterprise, and fall into unbiblical practices as a result. Many talk about particular places or regions as being very 'dark'. According to Scripture, if a place is clearly under the dominion of the powers of darkness, then the best thing we can do is plant local churches there and, in that way, the gates of Hades will not prevail. I have written much more about this in my book, *Demolishing Strongholds*.[13]

- **Discipling**
Because it is the most effective way of discipling people. Discipling has usually been seen primarily from the perspective of an individual's own personal sanctification and personal disciplines. Most western-based discipling manuals emphasise one-to-one discipleship; how an individual should pray, read the Bible, witness, etc. This is all very good but misses out a very important dimension of New Testament life. When Jesus was making disciples, he had to handle their disputes about who would be the greatest;[14] he brought together people as diverse as Simon the Zealot, a revolutionary who hated the occupation of the Roman soldiers, and Matthew, a tax collector, who had previously collaborated with the Romans. To make disciples, we need to bring different sorts of people together.

As I have written, the difficulties of church planting in the Middle East are often not just the problems of personal discipling, but of helping people to trust one another in a new community. In the New Testament, discipling was corporate. Many of the discipling chapters of the epistles refer to how we relate to one another. We cannot become effective disciples on our own, because an important key to our growth in Christ is how we relate to others. This, in turn, is not possible without a church and indeed a church composed of people from very different backgrounds, united in Christ.

In Colossians 3:1–11, Paul first encourages believers in their new position in Christ and then exhorts them to set their minds on the things above rather than the things on earth; they have now died with Christ and their life is hidden with him. He continues with issues of personal discipleship, urging his readers to deal with immorality and lust etc. However, he quickly moves on to issues that affect our relationships together: anger, rage, slander, lying to one another. He then returns to the truth that we have put off our old self with all these evil practices and are now being renewed. However, that renewal is immediately corporate in application – here 'there is no Greek or Jew, circumcised or uncircumcised, barbarian, Scythian, slave or free'. It would seem that he is addressing relationship issues in a church which does, in fact, contain Greeks, Jews, barbarians, Scythians, slaves and free men – in other words, a church composed of very different people. As he approaches the positive side of what we must put on in place of our previous practices, he lists qualities that are all to do with our relationships together: compassion, kindness, bearing with each other, forgiving one another, binding ourselves with love in order to promote unity, the peace of Christ ruling in our hearts because we are one body (Col. 3, see verses 12–15).

This is consistent throughout the New Testament, for example, the final chapters of the book of Romans. In the earlier part of this letter, Paul has argued for the truths of the Christian gospel, salvation by grace and justification by faith. He then describes our response to the grace of God and starts off with a passage which would be a key text for individual discipling. '. . . I urge you, brothers, . . . to offer your bodies as living sacrifices . . . Do not conform any longer to the pattern of this world, but be transformed by the renewing of your mind . . .'[15] However, Paul only spends three verses on our individual response to the grace of God. The result of not conforming to the world but being transformed, is shown immediately in the way we are to look at ourselves compared with other people. We are members of a body. We have to function according to our gift within that body.[16] The remainder of that chapter concerns the handling of our relationships together.

The next chapter speaks of our relationship to the authorities, but then returns again to our relationships with one another. Love for one another is the fulfilment of the law. In chapters 14 and 15, Paul is handling the vexed question of how Christians who have different views on various external practices should treat one another. He then brings it all together in what some would see as the key verse of his whole epistle, what he has been leading up to all along, 'Accept one another, then, just as Christ accepted you, in order to bring praise to God.'[17] How can we truly work out all these relevant aspects of our discipleship without this corporate dimension? I recognise it can be painful sometimes; building relationships with those I do not naturally get on with is costly. It is also evidence of genuine maturity in Christ when we are able to 'Accept one another'.

- ## Community reflecting the Trinity
Because Christian community expresses the heart of God. God himself exists in perfect community. The doctrine of the Trinity describes the essence of God as a personal loving Being. It was the prayer of Jesus that his people should reflect this unity[18] and, as we saw in the previous

chapter, this was understood as having major evangelistic impact, so that the world may believe that the Father sent Jesus into the world. God has always been looking for a people in the earth who can be a worshipping community, reflecting his glory to those around. In the Old Testament this was intended to be expressed through the people of Israel, but in the New Testament it is clear that this new people will be composed of those redeemed from every tribe and nation and language. Furthermore, this community, the people of God, must be visible, a city set on a hill that cannot be hidden.[19] A city suggests a corporate community, which the world can see, not just a few sanctified individuals, or a 'mystical concept' of Christian unity.

- **Presence of the age to come**
  Because churches are to be the eschatological community, demonstrating in this age the presence of the age to come. In the future age, after the return of Jesus, the dwelling place of God will be with men.[20] God is seen as dwelling in the new city, where there is no need of a temple because he himself is there.[21] The church's task is to demonstrate that future reality now, in the present age. Just as we are given the deposit of the Holy Spirit as a down payment guaranteeing our future glory as individuals, so the church is the down payment of the future glory of God dwelling with his people, who are even now being built into a temple in which God lives by his Spirit.[22]

- **Prophetic dimension**
  Because there is an important prophetic dimension to church planting. We are still seeking God for him to move again in revival power, as he is doing in some parts of the world. We do not just sit back, however,

passively waiting for revival. We work hard to win the lost for Christ and to establish churches with clear New Testament values so that when God moves in revival power and adds many new converts, they are added to a community. We want to have new wineskins ready for the new wine of God's Spirit.[23] We believe that God will do mighty things in the last days as the gospel of the kingdom goes to every people group, and therefore we seek to plant churches both to demonstrate God's idea of community now, and also in preparation for the blessing we anticipate.

Specific Prophetic Words

Church planting is thus based both on a vision from God and on New Testament teaching and practices. Many have had specific prophetic words about church planting, whether in our own nations or elsewhere. My friends, Edward and Fridah Buria in Meru, Kenya, have had a passion for the church expressed over many years. They have attended the same Bible Weeks as I have, hearing the doctrine of an end-time glorious church, and that has motivated them over the last five years to see over one hundred churches planted in Kenya, amongst different people groups, amongst tribal peoples as well as settled peoples.

The family of churches of which I am part has a commission from God to see 1,000 churches planted in the United Kingdom. Other groups of churches have a similar vision; for example, it is exciting to see how, amongst charismatic Anglicans, some previously redundant churches are having new communities of God's people effectively planted within them. We need to keep in mind, however, any such specific prophetic words and visions to particular groups or individuals are consistent with the promises of God in Scripture for an end-time glorious church. It is this big vision of what God wants to do in the earth, as well as the specific vision God may have given for a particular place, that sustains us in the difficulties of pioneering new churches.

Praise God, he gives us both; not only the big picture, but also specific vision and words of encouragement, as he did for Paul in the city of Corinth when he told him that he had many people in that city.[24] In order to church plant, there must be both the big vision of God's purposes in the earth, together with the specific direction of God's call to a particular place, to sustain us through difficulty and keep us in faith. It was obviously necessary in the case of the apostle Paul, because of the evident depression he struggled with at the beginning of his ministry in Corinth.

Spontaneity Then and Now

If we are to fulfil the vision God has given us for church planting, we need to recover the spontaneity and initiative of the New Testament believers. As they were scattered by persecution, or simply travelled around, they shared the gospel with unbelievers and planted new churches. Sometimes it was through an evangelistic campaign, as with Philip the evangelist in Samaria.[25] Sometimes it was people who are not even named sharing the good news as they were scattered;[26] sometimes it was people opening up their homes, like Priscilla and Aquilla,[27] so that churches could be started in them. In the New Testament, church planting was the result of the hand of God upon believers as they responded spontaneously to his Holy Spirit and exercised the gift of hospitality, so that churches were started in many houses.

Scattering may be similarly as a result of persecution today; the tense situation currently being experienced in Zimbabwe is causing many to leave the country for very understandable and sometimes essential reasons. Such action of change and scattering in turbulent times can lead to opportunities for the planting of new churches, just as in the New Testament. From River of Life Church in Harare, other churches have been planted by individuals going through personal times of change: 'Tapiwa Chizana (22) planted his church 6 weeks before his Accountancy Board Exam (and passed!) and remains a full-time accountant; Mbonisi Malaba (23) is a full-time practising doctor; Scott Marques (31) is a full-time businessman of a very large company; Sibs Sibanda (24) planted his church within 6 months of his marriage; and Innocent Charekera (31) is now a full-time church leader having been a gardener all his life. Leaders that model a missionary lifestyle reproduce after their kind.'[28] In other more rural parts of Zimbabwe, farms with Christian workers have been seized and the workers scattered. What some have done is to plant churches in the places to which they have been scattered.

Even in more propitious circumstances, we can be scattered for many other reasons. Some people may change jobs and therefore be scattered to other nations, or to other parts of their own nation. Why not use this opportunity to start a new church? Others sense the call of God specifically to go to a particular place.

What About the Totally Unreached

Church planting is essential as a strategy for preaching the gospel to people groups as yet unreached. Jesus told us to go and make disciples of every nation,[29] and this means more than obtaining one convert in every people group! As we have seen already, making disciples implies community. Jesus and his disciples were like a prototype church as they travelled together in community. Indeed, in many ways, that is a better picture of a church than a settled pastoral community. Rightly, therefore, an unreached people group is described as a people group without a reproducing church.

An unreached people group should be defined as 'a people group within which there is no indigenous community of believing Christians able to evangelise this people group without outside (cross-cultural) assistance'. 'Unreachedness' is thus not defined on the basis of whether there are any Christians or not, or whether there are any missionaries working among them or not. It is defined on the basis of whether or not in that culture there is a viable, culturally relevant, witnessing church movement – Ralph D. Winter.[30]

Personal Experience – Bedford to the Islamic World

When I received the prophetic word about planting churches in the Midlands area of England, I was already carrying in my heart an earlier prophetic word. In 1994, as in many parts of the world, we experienced an amazing move of the Holy Spirit in our churches in Bedford. During that time we had a visit from Steve Nicholson, who leads the Evanston Vineyard in Chicago. He travelled to us with a band of prophetic people and, at the end of one of the meetings when the Holy Spirit was moving very powerfully, one of these prophets addressed me publicly in the meeting and said that, one day, my ministry would affect the Muslim world. I had always taken an interest in world mission and I had devoured the books of missionary statesmen, often when I travelled around the world on business. However, I had not thought at all of my own ministry affecting Muslim countries. This prophecy came totally out of the blue as far as I was concerned. As these words were spoken to me, I fell to the ground under the power of the Holy

Spirit, with a deep conviction that it was God who was speaking. From that moment on, I knew that my eventual call was to be involved in that part of the world. But whatever our eventual call, it is important that we work hard at what God is giving us to do at the present time. So as a token of that prophetic word, I ensured that our early literature for The Midlands Initiative showed an arrow going from my home town of Bedford into the Midlands and then many arrows going out from there to other parts of the world.

Russia and Ukraine

It is also my joy to be involved in overseeing church planting in the former Soviet Union. Scilla and I travel often to those nations and God has joined us particularly to church planters in Russia and Ukraine. Recently, while we were in Eastern Ukraine, the leaders of one of the churches we are working with there took us around the villages and small towns of that region, where we were able to see the new churches that are being planted. It was so encouraging to meet churches which were becoming like a city set on a hill. One church we visited in a small town in Donetsk region had hired a former restaurant in the centre of the town, opposite the town hall, to hold its meetings and feed the hungry. They had asked the Mayor of the town to let them know names of the most deprived families for their kids' clubs. From that town, church planters were travelling out by bicycle to a nearby village to establish another church. Similarly in the Caucasus region of Southern Russia we are encouraging continuing church-planting zeal, including amongst unreached people groups. For those of us who were brought up with stories of the suffering underground church in the Soviet Union and the seeming impregnability of communism, it is very encouraging to see that now communism has fallen, church planting is a growing phenomenon.

I was recently talking to another friend in Ukraine. His passion, as a result of a vision from God, is to see drug addicts, alcoholics and former prisoners set free in the name of Jesus. He has therefore taken over a large old building in his town as a rehabilitation centre. It is wonderful to visit his church and see that many in his leadership team and worship team are former drug addicts or prisoners. This seems to add a particular vibrancy to the worship. The rehabilitation work had been his main concern, and he had not really been motivated by church planting until, at one of our conferences, he had become stirred by a vision for the church. As he was praying shortly afterwards, he felt God say to him, 'Why are you involved in seeing drug addicts set free?' He thought the answer was obvious but God pressed him again, and my friend suddenly responded in a new way: 'It is to have people available to plant new churches with, of course.' It has now become his vision to see new churches planted with teams of former drug addicts. In the villages around his home town, he is planting rehabilitation centres and embryonic churches together, in order to see the kingdom of God come to those villages.

As I talk to church leaders across Russia and Ukraine, I realise the costly nature of church planting there. For us in the west to go to small towns or villages is relatively easy in economic terms. For our Russian and Ukrainian friends, it means going to places where there is no work, where living conditions are very different from the larger towns and cities, and where alcoholism and drug addiction are rife. Nevertheless, the only way of bringing light into the darkness is to see communities of God's people indwelt by the Holy Spirit, established in these small towns and villages, and these church planters need to be willing to pay the price.

This is the New Testament method. This is what God will bless. It is often tougher than evangelism that is merely 'sowing seed', though I recognise that that, too, can be a tough and risky business. It must be our object right from the beginning to build genuine Christian community, as an alternative to what we find in the lands we go to. Greg Livingstone put it like this:

> Church planting is not necessarily a sequential operation. Even before Muslims confess Christ as their Saviour, they must be instilled with a notion that commitment to Christ (the Head) must include and involve commitment to Christ's body, the community of fellow believers. Without this conscious shift, adopting the other believers as brothers and sisters for whom they take responsibility, conversion is not complete. Conversion includes an internalising of allegiances, not only from whatever has been the highest authority in the Muslim's life to the Lordship of Christ, but also from blood relatives being first community to the new notion of Christ's community.[31]

Let Roland Allen have the final word on this. Again talking about Paul's preaching to heathen cities, he says:

> But he did not approach them as an isolated prophet; he came as an apostle of the church of God, and he did not simply seek to gather out individual souls from amongst the heathen, he gathered them into the society of which he was a member. He did not teach them that they would find salvation by themselves alone, but that they would find it in the perfecting of the body of Christ. Souls were not invited to enter into an isolated, solitary, religious life of communion with Christ; they were invited to enter the society in which the Spirit manifested himself, and in which they

would share in the communication of his life. It was inconceivable that a Christian taught by St Paul could think of himself as obtaining a personal salvation by himself. He became one of the brethren. He shared in the common sacraments. The church was not an invisible body formed of unknown 'believers'. Men were admitted by their baptism into a very visible society, liable to be attacked by very visible foes. The apostle who preached to them was a member of it, and he preached as a member of it, and as a member of it he invited them to enter it, to share its privileges and its burdens, its glory and its shame. ... St Paul's preaching ever appealed to and demanded the exercise of the two highest and deepest convictions of men, their sense of individual responsibility and their sense of social communion with their fellows.[32]

Notes

1 David J. Bosch, *Transforming Mission,* p. 117
2 Roland Allen, *Missionary Methods, St Paul's or Ours?* (Wm. B. Eerdmans Publishing Company, 1962), p. 5
3 Ibid. p. 3
4 1 Thessalonians 1:8
5 Acts 19:9,10
6 Colossians 1:7; 4:13
7 2 Corinthians 11:2
8 Ephesians 1:22,23
9 1 Corinthians 12:27
10 Philippians 2:15
11 Matthew 16:18
12 Ephesians 3:10
13 David Devenish, *Demolishing Strongholds* (Authentic, 2000), Chapters 4 and 7
14 Luke 9:46–48
15 Romans 12:1,2
16 Romans 12:4–8
17 Romans 15:7
18 John 17:21
19 Matthew 5:14

20 Revelation 21:3
21 Revelation 21:22
22 Ephesians 2:22
23 Matthew 9:17
24 Acts 18:9–11
25 Acts 8:5–7
26 Acts 8:4
27 Acts 18:26
28 Article by P.J. Smyth in November/January 2003 edition of *Newfrontiers Magazine*
29 Matthew 28:19
30 Ralph D. Winter, 'Unreached People: What, Where and Why?' An article in P. Sookhdeo (ed.) *New Frontiers in Mission* (Paternoster, 1987), pp. 146 and 149
31 Greg Livingstone, *Planting Churches in Muslim Cities* (Baker, 1993), p.13
32 Roland Allen, *Missionary Methods, St Paul's or Ours?* p. 76

Chapter Four

Church-Based Mission

One of the important debates in the modern-day church, particularly in terms of missiology, is the issue of the local church's responsibility for mission and therefore a questioning of the role of separate mission agencies. In 2003, Global Connections in the UK (the umbrella organisation to which most UK mission agencies belong) held a debate on the future of the mission agency, and in 2004 there was a consultation sponsored by Global Connections and the Evangelical Alliance on the church and global mission, at which I was asked to speak about church-based mission. My brief was to be as controversial as possible and to raise the very real issues concerning whether there is a future for mission agencies, now that the local church is beginning to take on its responsibilities for world mission.

There is a similar debate in the US. In 2003, I was asked to provide a commentary on a discussion paper provided by the missions magazine *Frontiers in World Mission*, on the subject of how mission structures should be governed. This raised the question as to whether the Bible provides us with information on the exercise of decision-making authority in how mission structures should operate. My comments were invited on a trend to the effect that: 'Brand new independent congregations are concluding that there is no need for mission agencies at all; each congregation should send out its own missionaries and global specialised mission structures are not legitimate or even necessary.' A missions elder in an American mega-church with a reputation for its commitment to world missions was quoted by way of example as saying, 'We didn't approve of what the missionary was doing, so we told him that he and his family had to return to the States.' A pastor of a large American church was said to have stated, concerning mission agencies, that there are numerous organisations who say their purpose is to be an 'arm' of the church – and that he prayed that the need for their existing would become obsolete because churches would obtain a healthy biblical perspective of ministry.

What is a Missionary?
Before even entering the debate on the responsibility and authority of a local church so far as its 'missionaries' are concerned, we need to consider, what is meant by the term 'missionary'? I approach this question with a certain ambivalence. On the one hand, I have been inspired throughout my Christian life by reading the stories of missionary pioneers. One of the first books I read after emerging from the claustrophobic and non-mission atmosphere of the Exclusive Brethren was the story of Jim Elliott who perished with his friends at their first encounter with the Auca Indians they had come to reach with the gospel. I always found it inspiring that though the deaths of the six godly young men seemed so pointless, yet through their example a greater number of young men and women volunteered for overseas

missionary service, and in particular, a greater concern was awakened for unreached tribes.[1]

My life has also been challenged by reading the story of Hudson Taylor and his dedication to serve the people of China by becoming as much like them as possible, thus exemplifying Paul's call for us to be slaves to all so that we may reach some with the gospel. I admired his persistence in calling out to God on Brighton beach for men and women to go to China, at a time when even the journey there was full of danger.

When our children were young, we spent time together for a few minutes round our evening meal, reading the story of C.T. Studd and his pioneer work in China, India and Africa. What a 'cloud of witnesses' we have as our examples, even since the days of the New Testament! Quite often when I am meditating upon the need all over the world for the gospel to go to the unreached, I will get out my copy of the excellent book *From Jerusalem to Irian Jaya*,[2] which contains short histories of different missionaries through the ages. I read just a few of the stories again to help me in my own dedication to the cause of the gospel of the kingdom going to every people group.

On the other hand, 'missionaries' often receive a mixed press. Contemporaries of mine who were brought up in mainstream traditional denominations, as opposed to my secluded existence, speak of the annual 'missionary weekends' that they felt obliged to attend, where the picture presented of missionaries was perhaps unjustly 'quaint'. My friends speak of sitting at the back to try and avoid 'getting the call' to mission work. And today, in the popular secular media, missionaries have received a bad press for allegedly undermining the indigenous cultures of tribal people by bringing them a 'foreign' religion. Amongst some younger people, therefore, the call to serve internationally in poverty relief or development can be more 'politically correct' or emotionally acceptable than taking the gospel to an unreached people.

The use of the term 'missionary', then, is certainly suspect, even amongst some of us committed to world mission. At one of our senior leaders' gatherings, where we brought together leaders from our churches from around the world, I presented a paper where I said that we, as a family of churches, needed to act like a 'missions agency' and recruit people from our churches to go to the unreached. The very uttering of the words 'mission agency' was like a 'red rag to a bull' for one of my African friends. When I asked him afterwards why he so objected to my use of that terminology, he said that in his mind, the idea of a mission agency conjured up two things:

- First, racism. He quoted the example of a mission agency in his own country, which had two sorts of accommodation at their conference centres, ostensibly just at different prices so that people could choose either basic or more luxurious accommodation. In his view, however, the reality was that one was for whites and the other for blacks.
- Second, he told me that he had observed in mission agencies in his country a lack of faith in the effectiveness of the gospel, resulting in explanations of why something couldn't be done, rather than an aggressive faith that would believe it could be done. How sad, bearing in mind the aggressive faith of many of the missionary pioneers.

This illustrates how our personal perspective, history and experience, affect the way we view particular terminology. On the other hand, many believers from countries who received the gospel in the last two centuries through visiting missionaries express real gratitude for what the missionaries brought, even though they do not in any way want to be dependent upon them. Some from Latin American countries, for example, are being sent by their churches to the UK, to what is now largely a humanistic and godless nation, in order to bring the gospel here, because of their gratitude for what British missionaries once brought to them. Indeed, a television documentary recently recorded a number of people from different parts of the world, who are now serving as missionaries in the UK.[3]

One of the difficulties is the word 'missionary' used as a noun rather than an adjective. I don't believe in missionaries as a separate group of people, I believe in a missionary church where all the members see themselves as sent into the world, and of these, some will be called to serve in other cultures or in other nations. The New Testament describes gifts and ministries of the Holy Spirit, and it would be helpful to use the biblical terminology as we consider the roles of those we send out.

- Some will be church planting *apostles*. The word 'missionary' is, in a sense, the Latin equivalent of the Greek word 'apostle', though certainly most so-called 'missionaries' would not claim to be apostles.
- Others will be *evangelists* who have a cross-cultural dimension to their evangelistic gift.
- Yet others will be *prophets* who clearly see the call to mission in our day as fulfilling the prophetic vision originally given to Abraham to see all the families of the world blessed. Such men and women are able to inspire many to have a global perspective and create a passion to reach the unreached. I believe there are those gifted in this respect who, over recent years, have called many into worldwide mission.

- Many others will be *helps*, those called to exercise gifts of service, who will assist indigenous church leaders through their medical or scientific experience, or will serve church planting apostolic leaders, as part of their teams, with gifts of administration through business acumen or computer skills.

How Did Mission Develop in the New Testament?

The next question we need to ask is how mission was developed in the New Testament. As we have seen before, the local church is essentially a missional community. I would define a local church as a grace-motivated, Spirit-filled community of people from all walks of life in a particular locality, who have a common faith in Christ and are committed to one another and to leaders who serve and care for them. That community is, however, missional at its core, understanding that its responsibility is to reach others with the gospel.

From the start, the church's mission was intended to be cross-cultural in nature. Jesus told them to go first to Jerusalem, then to Judea, then to Samaria, then to 'the ends of the earth'.[4] When the first church of 120 gathered in an upper room, that calling was clear to them. I believe the same calling needs to be integral to every church that shares that same New Testament DNA. I believe that for each local church, Jerusalem is the equivalent of their own town, Judea is the surrounding region where more churches can be planted, and Samaria represents those who are close to them geographically but different culturally. This 'Samaria' factor was a major one in New Testament times, not only with the Samaritans themselves, whom the Jews were prejudiced against because of their non-Jewish religious practices, but also in the great cosmopolitan cities of the Roman Empire, where many cultures rubbed shoulders together. It is a world very similar to our own in the twenty-first century, where increasingly people of different cultures live close to each other. There is finally to be within each local church a passionate intention to reach the ends of the earth and therefore become a 'sending' community.

Spontaneous and Strategic

New Testament mission was both spontaneous and strategic. The spontaneous occurred as believers were scattered from Jerusalem or Rome through persecution. However, there was also strategic mission, in particular the apostolic journeys led by the Holy Spirit. Paul describes his journeys thus: '. . . from Jerusalem all the way around to Illyricum, I have fully proclaimed the gospel of Christ'.[5] Illyricum is modern-day Albania and Croatia. However, whether the mission was strategic or spontaneous, those who went with that mission went from a local church and then planted churches.

New Testament mission was also church-based and oriented towards church planting. Once he had planted churches, Paul wanted to move on, leaving them to fill in the gaps in his evangelisation by reaching their own towns and surrounding areas. He could describe himself as having 'fully proclaimed the gospel' not because he had preached it to every individual in that vast area, but because he had left behind mission-minded churches who could take on that responsibility. As Roland Allen again says:

> St Paul's theory of evangelising a province was not to preach in every place in it himself, but to establish centres of Christian life [i.e. churches] in two or three important places from which the knowledge might spread into the country around. This is important, not as showing that he preferred to preach in a capital rather than in a provincial town or in a

village, but because he intended his congregations to become at once a centre of light. Important cities may be made the graves of mission as easily as villages. There is no particular virtue in attacking a centre or establishing a church in an important place unless the church established in the important place is a church possessed of sufficient life to be a source of light to the whole country around. . . . When he had occupied two or three centres he had really and effectually occupied the province.[6]

So mission was church-based and church planting oriented.

The Role of the Apostle

Furthermore, whether the mission was strategic or spontaneous, the role of the gift of the apostle was crucial. When Philip the evangelist went to Samaria and saw many saved and healed, it was still considered necessary for Peter and John, the apostles, to come down from Jerusalem to ensure there was a good foundation. They noticed (as did Paul in Ephesus some years later) that the new converts had not been baptised in the Holy Spirit.[7] They therefore laid hands on them and they were filled with the Holy Spirit. Similarly, when cross-cultural mission took place in Antioch and the new church was established, the church in Jerusalem sent down Barnabas who asked Paul to join him to teach and lay a good foundation in that church.[8]

So where did authority for the mission lie? With the local sending church or with the missionary team? Paul and Barnabas were clearly accountable to their sending church in Antioch; they returned and spent much time there, and gave an account to the church of what was going on in their missionary activity.[9] Paul was also clearly accountable to other apostles, though he retained an independent judgement and spoke out when he felt the purity of the gospel of the grace of God was being compromised by them, arguing the case for the inclusion of the Gentiles in the church in the council of apostles and elders in Jerusalem.

Paul was never independent of a local church, but joined to the local churches he planted whilst he stayed in particular places, and he wrote of these churches in terms that suggest a genuine family context; in 1 Thessalonians, for example, he described himself as being like both a father and a nursing mother.[10] He not only shared the gospel with the churches, but his life as well.[11] In other words, he was a part of the community of the church which he founded. There is sometimes a tendency in modern missions to discourage 'missionaries' from really becoming part of the local church community they are forming. That was certainly not Paul's practice. In no way did he stand aloof or apart. Again, when recalling his visit to Ephesus when he met with the Ephesian elders, it was evident that they knew what his life was like when he was there and could therefore base their leadership style upon his example. They were full of affection towards him and wept when he told them they would not see him any more.[12]

While he accepted accountability, however, Paul did not refer back to Antioch for instructions as to where he should go next. It was the Holy Spirit who prevented him from going into Bithynia or Asia, and it was as a result of a vision in the night that he sensed the call to go to Macedonia.[13] He did not refer back to Antioch at this point, but he did consult with the apostolic team who were travelling with him, and it is clear from the word 'we' that they took the decision together to go to Macedonia. Paul was not a loner, making all the decisions by himself, but rather the apostolic team functioned like a community on the move. Indeed, Paul hated to serve anywhere by himself. He refused to take advantage of an 'open door' in Troas because Titus had not yet arrived to work with him. Rather than begin a work without his team partner, Paul left Troas in search of him.[14]

The Apostle's Role Towards the Local Church

I believe that authority in a local church rests with the founding apostle until its local eldership is established. That local eldership will probably then choose, out of friendship and relationship, to continue to receive the benefit of that apostolic ministry, which then serves that local eldership and the church at their invitation.

As that continuing fathering apostolic role is received by a church, so the apostle seeks to involve that church in his wider mission. Paul, for example, encourages the church in Corinth to bring themselves into line with his apostolic advice, so that he can then move on to the regions beyond them.[15] It is a refreshing motive, probably not much referred to today, for a church to resolve its difficulties together, so that the apostle with fatherly care for that church can say goodbye to it and move on to others who have not heard the gospel!

The church in Philippi evidently helped Paul with financial support in his mission to Thessalonica.[16] When he was writing to Rome in anticipation of his visit there, Paul said he was coming in order that he might bless them, but also that they might assist him on his way to Spain.[17] The word used for 'assist' here does not just mean a prayer, but genuine support, financially and in other ways, for the ongoing mission. Paul also invited people from the various churches he served to join his apostolic team, thus recruiting new people to the cross-cultural mission.

Do Apostles Continue Today?

The problem we have in deciding whether authority in a local church rests with that church or with the mission agency that founded it, is that we have left out of our consideration the gift of the apostle. Apostles are gifts to the church[18] so they are not separated from the church, but have a particular role and authority within the church, or at least the churches they have founded. We need to distinguish clearly between two uses of the word 'apostle'. The first generation apostles have a unique status and authority, in that their teaching and writings form the New Testament Canon of Scripture, which cannot be altered or added to. We should not confuse that unique role of the first apostles with the ongoing need for apostolic ministry for the sake of church-planting mission. The New Testament is clearly the foundational document for doctrine and practice within the church for all time, and nothing that is contrary to the teaching of the New Testament is to be permitted in our church life. The Scriptures are all we need for life and doctrine. However, those same Scriptures, in my view, make it clear that the five ministries of apostles, prophets, evangelists, pastors and teachers, are necessary until the church comes to full maturity.[19] I do not believe this maturity will be fully achieved before Christ returns, and thus I believe that apostolic ministry and apostolic authority functioning within and serving the church, are essential for the mission to which God has called us.

The function and gift of the apostle was not just another term for the leader or 'president' of a particular denominational stream or hierarchy, but was in the church and served the church by:

- Planting and laying foundations in churches[20]
- Appointing elders in churches[21]

- Moving on to regions beyond, reaching the unreached, with a passion for those who have never heard the gospel, and thus involving the church in the wider mission[22]
- Bringing wisdom to bear on difficult situations[23]
- Ensuring the poor are remembered[24]

It is therefore clear that apostolic ministry is necessary for church-based mission and church-based social action.

Practical Outworking Today

How does this then work out in practice in mission in today's world? Let me try and give a few examples. As part of the international apostolic team of the Newfrontiers family of churches, I have responsibility for a number of new church plants in various nations. Some of those nations are largely unreached and we have sent church planting teams to them. In one such case in Central Asia, the team leader was sent from one of our churches in Surrey. He and his wife and family are supported pastorally by that church, cared for, looked after when they return on leave, and prayerfully supported. It is my responsibility, however, in an apostolic capacity, to ensure that good biblical foundations and strategy are in place in the church plant in Central Asia. For that purpose I will visit them from time to time and keep in touch concerning any particular difficulties they may be experiencing. However, the pastor of their sending church also has wider responsibilities than his own church and is part of my team that serves that part of the world. A lot of the 'hands-on' apostolic work is therefore done by him as part of my team, and I have full confidence in his ministry there. We bring our different gifts to bear in the situation. He keeps in touch with me on developments.

In another situation in a Muslim region of north-west Africa, there is another church plant which I have not yet personally visited. However, the regional leader in the UK who overseas the sending church in Cambridgeshire for the couple leading that church plant, has an excellent relationship with them and again, as a member of my apostolic team, oversees them and helps them lay good foundations there. He will also involve their sending church in supporting them pastorally.

Indigenous Leadership

As we send people to plant churches, some of those sent will emerge with apostolic gifts themselves, as will indigenous leaders who are raised up. We believe that apostolic ministries in various nations should also take the initiative to reach the unreached near to them. Hence Edward Buria, who heads up an apostolic base church for us in Meru, Kenya, does not need us to send team leaders to plant churches in the unreached people groups around him. He has been able to do that much more successfully himself from his own apostolic base church, but again, he is part of a team and functions as part of our Africa team. Similarly, our apostolic base church in Accra, Ghana, is reaching out to other people groups in that part of the world.

Local churches that are planted will have a style that reflects the local culture, and this is very important, as we will see in a later chapter. However, the foundational values reflect the apostolic input. There may be people sent out from the UK or elsewhere to serve in kingdom projects, mercy ministries and ventures such as micro-enterprise projects in nations where indigenous local leadership or apostolic ministry is already established. When that happens, those sent out ('missionaries' as we used to say), would serve under the authority of local leadership. Such expatriate workers serving those projects must be accountable to local leadership in the place where they are serving, and need to recognise that from the start. They are not primarily accountable to their home base church or to a missionary agency.

A Role for Mission Agencies?

So what, then, is the need for missionary agencies? Biblically, we should value and benefit from the gifts within the whole body of Christ and not allow any party spirit. In my view, therefore, it is essential to benefit from the gifts and experience of those who have had many years of cross-cultural ministry. However, it is also true, as we have seen biblically, that church-based, church planting apostolic teams should be initiating cross-cultural mission.

It is clear that some kingdom work cannot be done by a church, a family of churches, a denomination or stream, or an apostolic team on their own. In such cases, for example, the work of Bible translation, it is important that agencies like Wycliffe Bible Translators work alongside and serve the local churches. In the case of Wycliffe, this is their vision, and they carry it out effectively. In Newfrontiers, we certainly benefit from such relationships with agencies such as Wycliffe Bible Translators and Tear Fund. However, 'para-church' activity of this sort must genuinely serve the local churches and not compete against them, and should also be accountable to local leadership where it exists.

In a number of situations, we have been able to forge partnerships with agencies in which our family of churches and the particular agency can each contribute their strengths. So for example, the church plant in Central Asia that I mentioned earlier is actually being done in co-operation with a particular agency which has expertise in reaching Muslims with the gospel. We have benefited from their input, but it is clear that the apostolic foundation being laid in the church is our responsibility. In practice we have developed such a good relationship with those serving from this particular agency that when we all sit down together with the team and discuss the situation, we are simply each bringing our gifts to the table rather than there being any sense of competitiveness between us.

We have also sent people out from our churches who have joined a team from another agency for specific training purposes and then, with the full understanding, co-operation and agreement of that agency, once they have been trained, have severed direct connections with the agency and simply become a church planting team benefiting from our apostolic authority.

Visionary and Pastoral Leadership

What is important is that churches are served and churches are planted. Growing churches need dynamic leadership for their mission both locally and internationally. Sometimes a contrast is made between the pastoral model of leadership needed in a local church and the more visionary type of leadership required for missions work. We somehow have to marry these two different gifts, as was clearly the case in Scripture where all five ministries were needed to fully equip the church for its work. In a perceptive, amusing and challenging chapter in his book, *Leading Your Church to Growth*, Peter Wagner poses the question provocatively, 'Why Bill Bright is not your pastor'. His point is that Bill Bright is a visionary leader who founded Campus Crusade for Christ and therefore is unlikely to be held within the constraints of the pastoral ministry in a local church. Peter Wagner developed the theory of 'modality' – a static local church – and 'sodality' – a dynamic expanding mission agency. However, in that context, he quotes missiologist George W. Peters as follows as referring to, 'An unfortunate and abnormal historical development which has produced autonomous, missionless churches on the one hand and autonomous, churchless missionary societies on the other hand.'[25] Whether local church or mission agency, we must deal a death blow to the notion that a church exists to care for its own members but then sends missionaries to join mission agencies who can send them to other parts of the world. These 'missionaries' are often seen to be the more committed people, or those who cannot work out their calling within traditional church life. No, the whole church exists for mission, and whether mission agency or church leaders, we must orient churches in that direction.

Traditional church practice has separated mission from the church. A full history of this can be seen in David Bosch's outstanding volume, *Transforming Mission*[26]. Quite early in its history, once it became established as the 'official' religion of the Roman Empire, the church began to be seen as a pastoral rather than a missional community, with the monasteries, and later the travelling friars, as its mission arm. Even today, traditional church denominations retain a 'parish' mentality that would have originally seen their prime responsibility as being to care for that parish. Non-conformist churches may not have a parish but have a parallel model of a preacher caring for a congregation. The Methodists developed a circuit, which was originally evangelistic in intent, but quickly became pastoral. The new churches have recognised apostolic ministry, but there is a great danger that this apostolic ministry is seen simply as a description of those who 'care for the churches'. This results in an expectation that a local church will receive so many 'pastoral' visits from their apostle each year. All this encourages the church in the belief that it is simply a pastoral community and not a missional community.

Certainly, apostles serve existing churches inasmuch as they lay good foundations in churches and have the responsibility of the care of the churches.[27] It is clear that Paul was very much emotionally burdened by his care for the churches. However, this is not the sole or prime motivation for apostolic ministry, as it was not for Paul. He was passionate to reach those who had never heard the gospel. He was prepared to say to churches that they would never see his face again[28] because of the imperative of taking the gospel to other lands.

The traditional view of a church (or in the context of new churches, the distortion of apostolic ministry into a traditional model) is illustrated by the following diagram:

• Traditional view of church

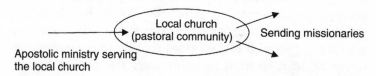

However, the New Testament view of the church is much more that of the mission-minded apostle functioning in and alongside a mission-minded church, so that both are involved in mission.

• New Testament view of church

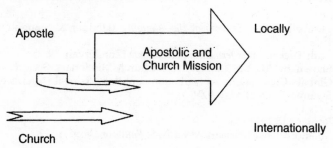

Churches are responsible for mission. They are responsible both at local and at international level and should therefore all seek to be involved in cross-cultural mission. Apostles and apostolic teams are gifts to the churches, who function within the churches and not separately from them, and have a prime responsibility for mission. They are sent ones. That is their whole raison d'être. Church-based mission and mission-minded churches are consistent with the foundation that Jesus laid in his church, as we have already seen in Chapter Two. The responsibility for church planting mission therefore is with apostolic ministry and local churches. Such mission takes place both strategically and spontaneously as people are led by the Holy Spirit. Those in mission agencies who have tremendous God-given vision, wisdom and experience in mission, need to find fresh ways of serving and helping local churches and apostolic teams in order to further the work of church planting mission. It is important that there is no sense of competition with local churches over the availability of those in a particular local church who want to be involved in cross-cultural mission. Rather those with experience in mission agencies can help the churches in fulfilling their calling.

Notes

1 Elisabeth Elliot, *Shadow of the Almighty* (Hodder & Stoughton, 1958)
2 Ruth Tucker, *From Jerusalem to Irian Jaya* (Zondervan, 1983)
3 Shown by Martin Thomas, rep. Church Missionary Society, at Global Connections consultation entitled 'Global Interface', Swanwick, 19–21 May 2004
4 Acts 1:8
5 Romans 15:19
6 Roland Allen, *Missionary Methods, St Paul's or Ours?*, p. 12

7 Acts 8:14–17
8 Acts 11:22–26
9 Acts 14:26–28
10 See 1 Thessalonians 2:7 and 11
11 1 Thessalonians 2:8
12 Acts 20:36–38
13 Acts 16:6–10
14 2 Corinthians 2:12,13
15 2 Corinthians 10:15,16
16 Philippians 4:14–16
17 Romans 15:23,24
18 Ephesians 4:11
19 Ephesians 4:11–13
20 1 Corinthians 3:10
21 Acts 14:23; Titus 1:5
22 2 Corinthians 10:15,16
23 e.g. 1 Corinthians 7
24 Galatians 2:10
25 Peter Wagner, *Leading Your Church to Growth* (Marc Europe, 1984), p. 146–7 quoting G.W. Peters, *A Biblical Theology of Missions* (Moody Press, 1972), p. 214
26 David J. Bosch, *Transforming Mission*, pp. 201–202
27 2 Corinthians 11:28
28 Acts 20:38

Chapter Five

Talking About the Kingdom of God

We have already seen that the missional church was a priority in Jesus' heart and mind before and after his death and resurrection. His other and equal preoccupation, however, was the kingdom. After his resurrection '. . . he showed himself to [the apostles he had chosen] and gave many convincing proofs that he was alive. He appeared to them over a period of forty days and spoke about the kingdom of God'.[1] Talking about the kingdom was the top priority for Jesus during the forty days he had with his disciples before his ascension to heaven. What days they must have been! Having meals together and talking about the kingdom!

The Old Testament, and particularly the 'Restoration' prophets to whom we have already referred, looked forward to a day when God would reign on earth. Isaiah prophesied concerning the Messiah: 'For to us a child is born, to us a son is given, and the government will be on his shoulders.' Then after listing the wonderful titles of the Messiah, he says, 'Of the increase of his government and peace there will be no end. He will reign on David's throne and over his kingdom, establishing and upholding it with justice and righteousness from that time on and for ever.'[2] This verse summarises the hopes of the prophets that are revealed time and time again in their writings. A kingdom is coming. A king will rule. Righteousness, justice and peace will be established.

Imagine, therefore, the sense of excitement and anticipation among godly Jews, who knew the prophets' writings so well, when Jesus came on the scene, announcing 'The kingdom of God is near',[3] and preaching the gospel of the kingdom. The apostle Paul, too, taught about the kingdom and looked forward to its eventual triumph in his great resurrection chapter: 'Then the end will come, when he hands over the kingdom to God the Father after he has destroyed all dominion, authority and power. For he must reign until he has put all his enemies under his feet. The last enemy to be destroyed is death.'[4]

Personal Journey to a Kingdom Understanding

It is important, therefore, that we have a kingdom theology as well as a church theology. Sadly, I believe many Christians have neither, but only 'a personal salvation' theology.

I vividly recall the time when I began to understand the significance of the doctrine of the kingdom of God. It was in the 1980s, when John Wimber's ministry was beginning to impact the charismatic church in the United Kingdom, across the traditional denominations as well as in the new church streams. Along with many church pastors and others, I had gone to a series of meetings led by John and his team in Westminster Central Hall. Though relatively new to this country, he had already had an impact upon David Pytches at St Andrews, Chorleywood, and David Watson at St Michael le Belfry, York.

I listened on the first evening to his hilarious personal

testimony and his account of his conversion and how he had personally encountered the Holy Spirit. Then after the teaching, something happened that most of us had not seen before. John Wimber simply and quietly invited the Holy Spirit to come amongst us. People started falling, crying out and shaking. There were words of knowledge for people with particular sicknesses and a 'clinic' took place on the platform where the people were prayed for and God's healing power was released. On that first evening, to be honest, my emotional and intellectual reactions were very mixed. I could not deny what I was witnessing; it seemed clear that God was at work, and there was no sense of manipulation. Yet I could not quite relate to what was going on around me. Travelling home on the train afterwards, leaders from another church in Bedford asked me what was wrong, since I did not seem to be excited about what I had seen in the way that they were. It was not that I was unexcited, I was simply thoughtful.

I returned to Central Hall the next day and John Wimber taught on the kingdom of God. He talked about the dynamic of the effective rule of God into people's lives, and how it was demonstrated through the healing and deliverance ministry of Jesus. As he spoke, revelation dawned for me. And as that truth of the kingdom revealed itself to my mind, so my spirit was affected, and this time, when John Wimber invited the presence of the Holy Spirit at the end of the meeting, I was overcome. I was deeply repentant over my cynical, over-analytical attitude to what, quite evidently, God was doing. I also understood for the first time how the reality of the demonstration of the Holy Spirit's power is linked with a clear theology of the kingdom of God. John Wimber frequently quoted George Eldon Ladd during his teaching, and I subsequently found Ladd's books on the subject extremely helpful for my own thinking.[5]

The kingdom of God is presented in Scripture as growing in the midst of the kingdom of darkness and eventually replacing it. The 'powers and authorities', which are presented in the New Testament as ruling in this world, will be defeated. The background to this thinking is to be found in the Old Testament, and in the book of Daniel in particular.

A King Has a Nightmare

Nebuchadnezzar was a great soldier and king, who ruled much of the world. Though he should have been someone who was able to sleep peacefully, night after night he had terrible dreams. In the morning, it seemed he could not remember his nightmares, yet the power and the fear of them remained with him. In fact, it later became apparent that God was speaking to the pagan king through these dreams, just as today God is speaking to many in Muslim and Hindu contexts through dreams about Jesus.

Nebuchadnezzar wanted his astrologers and 'wise men' to tell him what he had dreamed, as proof of their ability to supernaturally understand what the dream meant, and was furious when they were unable to do so. It was the young man Daniel, taken captive from the land of Israel, who offered to tell him the content and interpretation of his dream through God's revelation. Nebuchadnezzar had seen a huge and terrifying image of a man, its upper part made of gold, but its feet a weak mixture of iron and clay. This image represented the empires of the world which, though seemingly impregnable, would eventually fall. Into this picture, in Nebuchadnezzar's dream, came a tiny stone, cut out without hands. It struck the massive image and, though small, smashed it into fragments, which were scattered on the wind. The stone itself then became a mountain filling the whole earth. The empires of this world throughout history are seen here as cruel, terrifying and seemingly all-powerful. Yet all empires fall; all human rulers, however powerful, come to nothing. And the apparently tiny stone, the kingdom of God, continues to grow.[6]

Later, Daniel himself later had a similarly terrifying dream. He saw images of four fierce, grotesque animals; a bear with ribs in its mouth, a lion that could fly, a leopard with four heads, then something indescribably evil with iron teeth, trampling everything underfoot. As Daniel was thinking about this representation of evil, the vision suddenly changed. Daniel saw the throne of God, with a river of fire flowing from it and, sitting on the throne, the Ancient of Days, the God who exists and rules from eternity to eternity. Daniel was told that dreadful times would come, when demonically inspired governments, terrifying in their cruelty, would oppress God's people; yet the throne of God remains forever, and his kingdom will be established. The conclusion is, 'Then the sovereignty, power and greatness of the kingdoms under the whole heaven will be handed over to the saints, the people of the Most High. His kingdom will be an everlasting kingdom, and all rulers will worship and obey him.'[7] These are pictures of human history, worked out at all times, all over the world.

Cruelty By World Powers

The twentieth century, particularly, experienced the terrifying reality of man's inhumanity to man, inspired by demonic power, and for many Christians, the question of how to understand and react to unjust and evil governments and authorities can prove difficult. Indeed, there is a tension in the way Scripture itself views human government. On the one hand it teaches that 'the authorities that exist have been established by God.'[8] Even Pontius Pilate would have had no authority over Jesus unless it were given him 'from above.'[9] Yet on the other hand, the apocalyptic literature of Daniel and the book of Revelation view such governments as the haunt of unclean demons[10] and inhuman beasts capable of indescribable cruelty. The last century saw many manifestations of these beasts: two world wars; the evil of fascist dictatorships; exploitation by colonial powers; the beast of apartheid in Africa; the beast of cruel communist dictatorship which, under Stalin and Mao Zedong killed more millions even than Hitler's appalling genocidal policies in the Holocaust; genocide in Africa and the Balkans; so-called ethnic cleansing.

There are, as Daniel's nightmare makes clear, different degrees of cruelty. Not all governments are as bad as each other in this respect, though both totalitarian regimes and democracies are capable of evil, and both are infiltrated by the powers of darkness. Whilst I believe that democracy is the safest form of government for the world in which we live, I am under no illusions but that democratic regimes are also capable of injustice. The characteristic of the kingdom of God is not democracy but justice. Greater evil may well be perpetrated by those engaged in ethnic cleansing, like a Saddam Hussein in his dealings with the Shi'ites or the Marsh Arabs; nevertheless the horrifying pictures of the so-called 'liberators' behaviour in Abu Grabh prison similarly show the marks of demonic infiltration. Both capitalism and socialism are capable of exploitation of others, and it is within democratic as well as totalitarian nations that hundreds of thousands of unborn infants have been killed as the result of abortion policies.

Certainly these things constitute quite a nightmare – no wonder Nebuchadnezzar woke troubled and afraid!

Yet in the midst of all this, a stone has been cut out without hands, through the supernatural intervention of God. When Jesus came and said, 'The kingdom of God is near', that stone started to grow. The kingdom of God, the rule of Christ, will become a mountain that fills the earth, according to the promise in Daniel. How can a mountain fill the earth? Only in the way that Jesus described: in every village, every town, every city, every nation, communities of believers are to be established as a city set on a hill that cannot be hidden.[11] During the last century, particularly in what is called 'The South' (i.e. Africa, South America and parts of Asia) the kingdom of God has been growing in this way. Christianity is proving vigorous. It will fill the whole earth.

Defining the Kingdom

So what does 'the kingdom' mean? It is not a static place that you physically go into, like the United Kingdom. When I return from one of my travels abroad and enter Heathrow Airport, I physically enter the United Kingdom, but entering into the kingdom of God is not like this. To enter God's kingdom is to benefit from the rule of its king; it is to come in submission to the benevolent rule of King Jesus. Wherever the rule of Jesus goes, there is the kingdom. It is a dynamic, not a static, concept. If the sick are healed, the kingdom extends; as the demonised are set free, so the kingdom comes; as good news is brought to the poor, so the kingdom of God is expressed; as justice comes into situations of injustice, so the kingdom of God is growing. Wherever God is obeyed, his kingdom comes. The kingdom is his will being done on earth as it is in heaven.[12]

God is sovereign, so ultimate authority belongs totally and only to him. Humankind was appointed to fill the earth and rule it in accordance with God's will, but because humanity sinned, Satan was allowed to become the 'prince of this world'[13], dominating the affairs of humanity as an impostor. Jesus has defeated the prince of this world through his cross and resurrection with the result that he now reigns in the world, though we do not yet see everything totally under his authority. He is reigning until all his enemies are under his feet.[14] 'We see Jesus, who was made a little lower than the angels, now crowned with glory and honour...'[15] After his resurrection, he said, 'All authority in heaven and on earth has been given to me'.[16]

However, it is the responsibility of the church, through its mission, to go and implement that authority. How? By making disciples of all nations until 'this gospel of the kingdom [is] preached in the whole world as a testimony to all nations, and then the end will come.'[17] As we do that, we become what we are intended to be, light to the world, salt for the earth (preserving and giving taste). The mountain of God's kingdom will grow. It will be lifted above other mountains. It will fill the earth. It is clear that it is a continually growing kingdom.[18]

Misunderstanding the Kingdom

In Jesus' day, as in ours, there were misunderstandings about the kingdom and what it meant. The Jews of Jesus' day were looking for a political kingdom, ruled by a political Messiah who would drive out the Romans. They imagined that when the kingdom came, the Jews would be made top nation, with all other nations serving them; that is how they interpreted prophecies such as Isaiah 60. When Jesus fed the 5,000, they really thought their time had come.[19] It is recorded that after this miracle, they tried to make Jesus king.[20] After all 'an army marches on its stomach', and a king who could miraculously feed his army on a few loaves and small fish could very easily

overcome the logistical problems that so often hinder
military campaigns.

When these false hopes for a political kingdom were
not realised, disappointed questions were asked. John the
Baptist, depressed by his imprisonment under Herod –
not what he had expected when the kingdom was
coming – sent messengers to ask Jesus, 'Are you the
one'.[21] Even after the momentous event of the resurrection, the disciples were still asking the wrong question:
'Are you at this time going to restore the kingdom to
Israel?'[22] However, Jesus had been teaching throughout
his ministry that his is a very different sort of kingdom.

Peace Not Force

It is not a kingdom of physical force but a kingdom that
demonstrates the power of peace, the power of forgiveness, the power of grace, the power to set people free from
the captivity of Satan and break the hold that Satan has on
people's lives through sin. We will return to this theme in
the next chapter, but I recommend we weigh in the context
John Stott's very important comments on this issue.

> It is important to remember that his promise that they
> would receive power was part of his reply to their question
> about the kingdom. For the exercise of power is inherent in
> the concept of a kingdom. But power in God's kingdom is
> different from power in human kingdoms. The reference to
> the Holy Spirit defines its nature. The kingdom of God is his
> rule set up in the lives of his people by the Holy Spirit. It is
> spread by witnesses, not by soldiers, through a gospel of
> peace, not a declaration of war, and by the work of the
> Spirit, not by force of arms, political intrigue or revolu-
> tionary violence.[23]

Broader Than the Church

Another misunderstanding about the kingdom is the idea that 'the kingdom is the same as the church'; that all 'kingdom' amounts to is the truth that we are individually born again, receive our personal salvation and then seek to live godly lives as part of the church. This inward-looking view of the Christian gospel is, in my view, a major hindrance to the church effectively demonstrating the kingdom. It leads to an individualistic piety, which is not sufficiently concerned for social issues. The kingdom is much wider than the church. The rule of God will affect the world, and will bring social justice.

But Not Separate From the Church

Another misunderstanding, however, is to make too great a separation between the kingdom and the church. Some who rightly have a prophetic vision for the kingdom of God and for the political and social action that their vision necessitates, become disillusioned with the church and seek to work out their kingdom vision elsewhere. They may still attend church, but the church has little bearing on their kingdom vision. Thus they see the kingdom in terms of politics or the fight for justice and social action, and see the church as non-political and merely a pastoral community. This can lead to frustration both ways. Those who are preoccupied with the kingdom become frustrated with what they perceive as the inward-looking nature of most churches; they hear sermons that relate only to life within the church community, instead of affecting the way we live in the world. At the same time, there can be frustrations for those preoccupied with discipling people within the church; they perceive a lack of interest or involvement in church life on the part of those who seem to have a much broader agenda.

Now and Not Yet

A further misunderstanding of the kingdom relegates the doctrine of the kingdom entirely into the future. This was the teaching I grew up with. Indeed, Dispensationalism properly understood postpones the kingdom completely until the kingdom age, after the church has been 'raptured'. It teaches that because the Jewish nation largely rejected the teaching of the kingdom that Jesus brought, we now simply preach the gospel of the grace of God and not the gospel of the kingdom, which is a future promise. The result of this again is a withdrawal from the world and a focus on one's own personal salvation.

It is perhaps not surprising that these misunderstandings arise, since there is a clear tension in the biblical teaching of the kingdom. The kingdom is spoken of in two ways – 'now' and 'not yet'. The kingdom has come, yet the kingdom is coming. We enjoy the kingdom now, yet we are waiting for the kingdom to be expressed in all its fullness. This can be expressed diagrammatically as follows

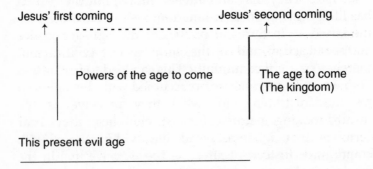

At present we are still living in what the Bible calls this 'present evil age'.[24] The kingdom has already come, but it will only come in its fullness after Jesus returns and brings in the 'kingdom' or 'the age to come'. However, as

the kingdom grows now, we are bringing into this present evil age the powers of the age to come, the powers of the now-reigning Christ. When we extend the kingdom we bring, as George Eldon Ladd puts it, 'The presence of the future'.[25] In the future there will be no sickness; so as we pray for the sick and they are healed, the presence of the future kingdom comes now. In the future kingdom there is no poverty, for all will have enough to eat and will dwell in security under their own vine and their own fig tree;[26] so as we feed the poor, we bring the future kingdom into the 'present evil age'.

> The presence of God's kingdom in Jesus was concerned not only with the spiritual welfare of men but also with their physical well-being. The kingdom of God . . . will mean the redemption of the complete man, thus requiring the resurrection of the body and a transformed natural and social order. We have seen that the miracles of healing were a pledge of this ultimate eschatological redemption. The kingdom of God is concerned with the evils that bring misery and suffering on the physical level. In these principles is implicit a 'social gospel', for the reign of God in the lives of his people must be concerned with the total man and with the conquest of evil in whatever form it manifests itself. The church is the people of God, the instrument of the kingdom of God in conflict with evil.[27]

So what are our expectations of the kingdom? Until Christ returns, there will always be a 'not yet' about our kingdom experience. Disease will remain, so not all will be healed. Poverty is not totally eliminated, so the poor will always be with us,[28] and always need our care. Yet the kingdom will grow and will have influence in every nation, and we will see Christian action against injustice.

However, because we live in this present evil age, the

kingdom of darkness will grow in influence unless we maintain our diligence in extending the kingdom of God. We are living in a time of 'kingdoms in conflict'.[29] If the church does not persist in being salt and light to society, evil increases. Indeed the Bible makes it clear that evil will increase; the spirit of antichrist is at work[30] until the final manifestation of the antichrist.[31] Persecution and tribulation will abound, yet we will also see the peace of the kingdom coming as we pray. Slavery may be abolished by Christian leaders with a passion for social action, such as William Wilberforce, yet slavery can still re-emerge, as has happened in some parts of the world, and economic slavery and new forms of social injustice can develop. So we see that the kingdom truly is both 'now' and 'not yet'.

Sometimes this doctrine of the kingdom, not properly understood, can make Christians passive. They simply say, 'Well, the kingdom has not come in all its fullness, so we cannot do much about it.' However, we are intended to be those who are actively engaged in praying and acting so that the kingdom comes.

Church and Kingdom

So what is the relationship between the church and the kingdom? They are not the same; the kingdom is bigger than the church, but the church is part of the kingdom. In talking about the church in this context, I am not just talking about church meetings or church organisation. Indeed in the New Testament we never find the expression 'going to church', rather we hear of 'when you come together'.[32] We are part of God's new community all the time. When we are at home, when we go to work in our secular jobs – wherever we are, whether gathered or apart – we are still the church.

The church, however, is the **witness** to the kingdom.

Jesus said to Peter in the context of building the church, 'I will give you the keys of the kingdom'.[33] We bring people into the kingdom through their acceptance of our message. The Twelve and the seventy-two were sent out to preach the good news of the kingdom.[34] Evangelising is not different from building the kingdom; it is a priority way in which we extend the kingdom. The gospel is good news to the poor.

The church is the **agent** of the kingdom. When Jesus was here on earth, he was the bringer of the kingdom. Now it is the church that is the means by which God's rule is extended through the world. The church is the agent of God's mission on earth. What is that mission? To preach the gospel of the kingdom and eventually to bring all things under the dominion and headship of Christ – 'to bring all things in heaven and on earth together under one head, even Christ'.[35] Though this will be complete only after Christ's second coming, our mission must be consistent with God's purpose and Christ's mission. Hence the church is always seeking to establish the kingdom in the world.

How does the church seek to establish the kingdom in the world?

- By prayer – 'your kingdom come, your will be done on earth as it is in heaven'[36]
- By evangelism – being born again into the kingdom[37]
- By the integrity of our lives – we are 'salt of the earth'
- By prophetic social action – bringing good news to the poor, seeking to bring justice to those who are suffering from injustice, being advocates for those who have no voice of their own.

In addition, the church as a community must prophetically **demonstrate** the kingdom. We must live according to kingdom values. It is impossible for us to engage in large social action projects for the poor with integrity, if we do not care for the poor amongst us. One of the Old Testament promises concerning the kingdom was the year of Jubilee, yet the principle of Jubilee was never fulfilled in Old Testament times. However, when the Holy Spirit fell on the church, it could be said: 'There were no needy persons among them'.[38] Kingdom jubilee had been demonstrated within the community of God's people. What could not be fulfilled by the law was fulfilled in a community indwelt and empowered by the Holy Spirit.

Also, the church must live out the kingdom **in practice**; the standards of the Sermon on the Mount must be our standards both as a Christian community and as individuals. We are continually encouraged in the epistles to exhort one another to a godly life, and even church discipline is to be a way of expressing the gracious reign of Christ to those who sin. We are not to be divisive and make major differences over minor issues, according to Paul. Our adherence to the things expressed in this chapter illustrate true kingdom life. Paul says very clearly, 'For the kingdom of God is not a matter of eating and drinking [i.e. just minor matters on which there can be legitimate differences], but of righteousness, peace and joy in the Holy Spirit'.[39]

What, therefore, does the kingdom affect?

- It affects sickness as the power of God is demonstrated in signs and wonders. Paul says, 'the kingdom of God is not a matter of talk but of power.'[40]
- It affects spiritual warfare. Demons being cast out of those being oppressed is evidence of the kingdom. 'But if I drive out demons by the finger of God, then the kingdom of God has come to you.'[41]
- It affects poverty. The church is to be generous to the poor, to help the poor have the dignity of work, to

bring justice to the poor and help the poor find their resource in God as well as in the Christian community. Thus the future kingdom is demonstrated by effects of the curse of poverty being broken now.

- The kingdom affects how we do our daily work. Our job description at work is to bring the kingdom of God. Again we will look at this in a later chapter. Bill Hybels puts it this way, 'When the true Christian enters the market place, Christ enters with him or her and together they must leave their mark of holiness.'[42]
- It affects racial issues. The curse of separation between races at Babel was turned to blessing as prophetically demonstrated at Pentecost.
- It affects ethical issues such as the church's action on abortion, on slavery, speaking out on euthanasia, campaigning on issues of injustice, seeking to bring the true liberation of women into their God-given dignity.

The kingdom is also to be our top priority. Jesus said, '. . . seek first his kingdom and his righteousness, and all these things will be given to you as well.'[43] The kingdom is to have far greater priority in our lives than concern about material things or anything else. It is to be top priority for the church in mission today. We want to see the kingdom built in the midst of the effect of the beasts of world empires, amidst totalitarian regimes, and we want to bring it in God's way, the way of peace, according to Jesus' own radical message in the New Testament, as we will see in the next chapter.

Notes

1 Acts 1:3
2 Isaiah 9:6,7

3 Mark 1:15
4 1 Corinthians 15:24–26
5 George Eldon Ladd, *The Gospel of the Kingdom* (Paternoster Press, 1959); George Eldon Ladd, *The Presence of the Future* (SPCK, 1974)
6 Daniel 2:26–45
7 Daniel 7 – concluding with v. 27
8 Romans 13:1
9 John 19:11
10 Revelation 18:2
11 Matthew 5:13–16
12 Matthew 6:10
13 John 16:11
14 1 Corinthians 15:25
15 Hebrews 2:8,9
16 Matthew 28:18
17 Matthew 24:14
18 Isaiah 2:2
19 John 6:10–14
20 John 6:15
21 Matthew 11:3
22 See Acts 1:6
23 John Stott, *The Message of Acts* (IVP, 1994), p. 42
24 Galatians 1:4
25 George Eldon Ladd, see above
26 Zechariah 3:10
27 Ladd, see above, pp. 303–4
28 John 12:8
29 Matthew 24:7
30 Implied by John's assertion of 'the antichrist' and 'many antichrists' in 1 John 2:18
31 2 Thessalonians 2:7
32 1 Corinthians 11:18,33; 14:26
33 Matthew 16:19
34 Luke 9:1,2; 10:1,9,11
35 Ephesians 1:10
36 Matthew 6:10
37 John 3:3,5
38 Acts 4:34
39 Romans 14:17
40 1 Corinthians 4:20
41 Luke 11:20
42 Bill Hybels, *Faith in the Real World* (Hodder & Stoughton, 1982), p. 2
43 Matthew 6:33

Chapter Six

The Kingdom Down to Earth

In Jesus' time, as we have seen, godly Jewish people were looking forward to the coming of the kingdom of God. Old Testament prophecies had spoken about the coming Messiah who would usher in God's rule upon earth. Then when Jesus came he announced that the kingdom of God was near. People saw the evidence of it: the sick were healed, water was turned into wine, demons were cast out, 5,000 were fed. It is easy to imagine the sense of anticipation. As well as being hungry for his miracles, the crowds that followed Jesus would have been expecting that any moment, the Romans would be overthrown and they would see the new, powerful kingdom of God established.

But Jesus then started behaving in ways that did not fit in with their preconceptions. He went to parties with 'sinners', and allowed a prostitute to wash his feet with her tears at a respectable dinner party in the house of Simon the Pharisee.[1] He did not seem concerned with keeping Old Testament rituals such as the washing of hands and Sabbath observance.[2] And he refused to be made king.[3] Indeed, some of his teaching went com-

pletely counter to any prospect of the overthrow of the
Roman yoke. The Jewish people would have deeply
resented certain rights claimed by the occupying force.
We can get some idea of how they might have felt by
observing the reaction of people of our own time whose
land is occupied by an 'invading' (or 'liberating' – depending on your perspective!) army. The Roman soldiers had
the right to demand of a Jewish man that he carry a
burden for the soldier for one mile. Jesus, rather than
calling on people to rise up against this injustice, said,
that when asked to do this, you should offer to carry it
two miles.[4] As we saw in an earlier chapter when the
people in his home town, Nazareth, listened to Jesus'
teaching, they were furious that he spoke about God's
blessing to the nations around instead of their
overthrow.[5]

Upside Down Kingdom

Jesus then spoke about the kingdom in terms far
removed from those of a military takeover. He said the
kingdom is like a farmer sowing seed[6] – hardly a picture
of a victorious military campaign! The kingdom is like a
tiny mustard seed,[7] or like putting yeast in flour to bake
bread.[8] The kingdom is finding treasure in a field and
being so excited that you sell everything else in order to
obtain the field.[9] The kingdom is like going fishing![10]

What was Jesus talking about? Even his own disciples
found his teaching on the kingdom puzzling, and as we
saw earlier right up to the time of his ascension, they
were asking, 'Lord, are you at this time going to restore
the kingdom to Israel?'[11] What was going on? We know
some of the answers.

• The people of Israel had failed to fulfil God's intention
  for them to be a light to the nations around. They had

become inward-looking and nationalistic, seeking to separate themselves from the nations around by ever-increasing ritual purity; and yet had fallen into serious sin themselves as a nation. Jesus came to fulfil God's original promise to Abraham and his descendants that through them all the families of the earth would be blessed. The kingdom of the Messiah would therefore be very different from what Jesus' contemporaries envisaged. The Gentiles were not to be overthrown, but blessed with the message of the good news of the kingdom of God. Jesus had come with a message of peace and goodwill to all people. He had not only taught this radically different message but predicted that God would vindicate it both by raising and exalting Jesus himself, and by bringing judgement upon those who rejected the message, such that not one stone would be left upon another in the temple, that pinnacle of Jewish nationalistic aspirations.[12] The kingdom would then be given to a people who would produce the fruit of the kingdom.[13] Those listening might have been thinking only of Israel; Jesus was thinking of the whole world.

- To establish this kingdom, Jesus had to defeat Satan, the prince of this world, at the cross. The real enemy – not the Romans but the sin of the human race – would be atoned for by Jesus' own death as a substitutionary sacrifice. Our sins were punished in Jesus, so that we could receive His righteousness and the amazing blessing of freedom from the penalty and the punishment which our sins deserve. All the forces of darkness, opposed to our freedom from the power of sin, were to be defeated at the cross and made a public spectacle.[14] The freedom of access into the presence of God, of which the old temple system could at best be a shadow,[15] would now be guaranteed through the crucifixion and resurrection of Jesus.

- Furthermore, instead of Jesus establishing the kingdom in one fell swoop, those who were willing to follow this new king and receive his message, were to be involved in bringing the kingdom to the whole world and thus blessing all the families of the world. The gospel of the kingdom would be preached in every people group, and only then would the end come.[16] So the kingdom and mission are integrally linked together. Our mission is the message of this very different, 'upside down' kingdom. There will be a new people who will inherit this kingdom, drawn from every people group.

Parables of the Kingdom – What Do They Teach Us?

The stories about the kingdom told by Jesus in Matthew's gospel, chapter 13, therefore have an immediate impact and relevance to the reception of Jesus' message at the time, but are also of help and encouragement for us today who are seeking to accomplish kingdom mission.

I believe that an understanding of these parables helps each one of us to get involved in the mission of the kingdom. We can all do simple things like sowing seed, or putting yeast into the dough. It also helps us cope with the frustration of delayed fulfilment, for which these parables help us understand the reasons.

The Sower

Firstly, Jesus told a parable about a man going out to sow seed. At that time (as in many parts of the world today), the fields would be criss-crossed by paths, and in many places, rocks would lie just under the surface of the soil. Sowing took place before the rains came, so that when the rain actually fell on the field, not only would the wheat germinate and spring up, but so would weeds, whose seeds were already in the earth, invisible until they sprouted.

One of the difficult things about this story is that Jesus said that he was speaking in parables so that people would *not* understand.[17] Yet parables are surely to help people understand. Often that is the case as, for example, when Jesus taught us not to worry about money by telling us a parable concerning God's provision for the birds.[18] However, by the time Jesus was speaking these parables of the kingdom, many people were amazed at his miracles and fascinated by his teaching, but unwilling to change their lives. Not only were they unwilling to repent of personal sin and follow Jesus but they were also unwilling to repent of their inadequate understanding of the coming of the Messiah. They had begun to be offended by a Messiah who was not promoting a political programme. Jesus therefore began to teach in parables which people could only understand if they were willing to follow him. Those who genuinely followed were given an explanation. As we follow, we learn more. This is what is meant by the 'mystery' of the kingdom. A 'mystery' in the New Testament is not something that we can never find the answer to, but something that requires revelation, and as we follow Jesus, revelation is given.

So what is Jesus teaching through this parable of the sower? That as the message of the Christian gospel is shared around the world, people will respond in different ways.

- Some people make *no* response. Before the seed penetrates, birds take it away. This means that there is spiritual warfare involved, because it is the evil one that takes the seed away; so we must pray as we sow.
- Others make only an *emotional* response. As the local church engages in mission, we see this so many times.

People who rush to the front to respond to the gospel, the early 'keenies' on our Alpha[19] courses, seem so excited about this new message of the Christian faith. Then difficulties arise; perhaps issues from their past lives, difficult personal circumstances, opposition from families or others, or even a failure to understand that Jesus is not primarily promising us personal blessing or easier circumstances, but is calling us to difficult and costly mission to this world. In the face of such circumstances, an emotional response is found to be insufficient.

- Others make a *preoccupied* response. The ground of their lives is literally occupied already by other seeds. People receive the word but are so busy, or so materialistic, or have so many family obligations or other commitments that the word is choked and cannot grow.
- There will also be the 'good ground' of those who make an *understood* response. These people see that the kingdom of God is the most important thing in the world, and that they need to bring their lives into line with it.

As sowers of the word of the kingdom, as those who explain the gospel, we need to understand the implications of this teaching. We cannot repeal the parable of the sower; this is how the kingdom is. As we share the gospel we will always find these four different responses, and quite often those who initially respond positively can be those who do not stay the course, so we need to sow lots of seed.

Application Today

A few years ago, I was overseeing the work of a full-time evangelistic team who were evangelising some of the estates of our town. Often they would find that certain people received them well into their homes and therefore most of their time as a team would be taken up with revisiting them. Many were needy people, and it was important to meet their practical needs as part of our gospel outreach. However, each week as we met together to review, I would ask the questions, 'But how many *new* houses have you visited?' 'How many *new* people have you spoken to?' We must keep sowing seed into new areas because we do not know at the outset where the good ground will be, or where there are in fact rocks under the soil.

It is also important that we aim for good ground. 'Good ground' is those who truly understand. We therefore need to make sure that people develop a clear understanding of what the gospel is and what its implications are in terms of the kingdom of God. In this way, we minimise the risk of a merely emotional response to a perception of needs being met. When Jesus called his original disciples, the promise from the beginning was that they would be fishers of men. 'At the beginning of the story, when the 12 whom Jesus appointed can understand themselves only as disciples, that is, as students of Jesus, their ultimate purpose was already stated by the evangelist; they would become apostles, sent out ones'.[20]

This parable also applies to how each of us hears the word of God at any time. I wonder how many messages many of you reading this book have heard! As Christians we often respond emotionally and then, when difficulties arise, forget all we have been taught and fall into sin or apathy.

The Weeds

Jesus then taught a parable about weeds. The truth about the kingdom of God is sown and starts producing fruit.

But, whilst the sower sleeps an enemy comes. Incidentally, sleeping is not regarded here as a bad thing; it is what you do after a hard day's work! However, when we are doing the work of the kingdom we need to understand that because the kingdom has not yet come in all its fullness, an enemy is at work as well. There will be warfare. The good will grow, but the work of the enemy will often grow as well. The field, says Jesus, is the world. As the kingdom grows, evil will increase as well.

The enemy is deceptive. The weed Jesus was speaking of was probably darnel, which looks very much like wheat in the early stages of its growth, and so is hard to identify until harvest time, when its lack of fruitfulness becomes clear. What are we to do about the 'weeds' of the enemy's work? Should we try to pull them all up? No, because destroying it may destroy the growth of the good as well. We need to understand that it is going to be like this right until the end, until the gospel has gone to every people group; otherwise we will become very frustrated. However, at the end all will be made clear and the fruitfulness of the wheat will be apparent.

Mustard Seed and Yeast

Jesus then told two parables which are particularly helpful to us today. The kingdom, he said, is like something that has a very small beginning, but grows to a great size. It is like a mustard seed which is very tiny yet produces a large tree. It is like yeast, which when put into the dough seems insignificant, but affects the whole loaf. The work of Jesus himself was like that. Only a few people were built into the new nation, the church, by the time Jesus had finished his ministry. We could view it as a leadership team of twelve, or a committed company who met together of 120, or 500 somewhat more dispersed disciples. If we were playing a numbers game, then the ministry of Jesus would not rate very highly in the history of the growth of mega churches. Yet his ministry was just like the mustard seed; it started small, but Christianity is now to be found all over the world. We may only be able to make a seemingly insignificant contribution to the work of the kingdom, compared with the huge tide of unrighteousness and ungodliness and injustice in the world. Yet it is a principle of the kingdom that if we make our small contribution, it will grow and eventually have a wide effect.

Pearl and Treasure

Jesus also taught parables to illustrate the high priority the kingdom should hold in our lives; it is more valuable than any other activity in which we could be engaged. They are the stories of a merchant looking for pearls and a man finding treasure in a field. For the joy of obtaining what they had sought for years, it was worth selling everything. This must be our attitude to the kingdom in our church-based kingdom activity. The kingdom is worth giving up everything for, and to do so is not irksome but a great joy.

It is often during times of persecution that Christians truly understand what these parables mean, and discover the joy of the kingdom. One of the most powerful stories from the suffering church during communist times was when Richard Wurmbrand writes about his time in solitary confinement in a Romanian jail. Amongst the other remarkable experiences, he records, 'The Communists believe that happiness comes from material satisfaction; but alone in my cell, cold, hungry, and in rags, I danced for joy every night . . . Sometimes I was so filled with joy that I felt I would burst if I did not give it expression.'[21] One of my Russian pastor friends told me how, during the time of the underground church in the

Soviet Union, his mother used to set off on Saturday evening and walk through the night to reach the place in the woods where the Christians were meeting on Sunday morning. It was important not to miss a meeting or you would not necessarily find out where they were meeting the following week!

It is difficult for those of us living in western affluence, with little obvious persecution, to find an equivalent to the pearl and the treasure, but the kingdom must be this precious to us. My experiences are so small compared to those who have suffered so much. I remember that in my mid-twenties, when I worked for a British government department, I was offered a promotion if we were willing to move to South Wales. If I had accepted the promotion, I would have been the youngest person in that department ever to reach that position. To be honest, because of my personality, that achievement was much more of a temptation than the increased salary! However, we had just started a new church in Bedford a few months previously, so I turned down the promotion.

Do You Understand?

Matthew ends chapter 13 of his gospel, from which these stories are taken, by quoting the urgent question Jesus put to his disciples after all this teaching: 'Have you understood all these things?' They said 'Yes', though later they showed they had still not really grasped the radical nature of the kingdom! However, if we are to understand the mission of the church, we must ensure that we are beginning to grasp the nature of the kingdom. The next verse (v. 52) is difficult to translate. *The Message* translation says, '. . . every student well-trained in God's kingdom . . .' A literal translation would begin, 'Every scribe discipled into the kingdom of the heavens.' I believe this is almost the key verse in the chapter. Why has Jesus taught these stories to his disciples? So that they can teach others; so that they can pass on to all nations the understanding of this new fresh view of the kingdom. We become disciples of Jesus in order to bring benefit to others. We therefore can offer people both the old treasure of the Old Testament prophetic hopes of the kingdom, and the new treasure of implementing the kingdom in the way that Jesus was introducing.

How Do These Stories Help Us?
The teaching of these parables in Matthew 13 helps us in a number of ways to develop a clearer and more 'down to earth' understanding of the kingdom.

Involvement
Firstly, it encourages us that we can all be involved. We may not think we can do great things in terms of changing the world, but we can all sow seed; we can all share our faith; we can all do acts of kindness and seek to bring justice into situations in which we find ourselves, being assured that each act of the kingdom will produce growth. We may not see the effect of this growth immediately, or even within our own lifetime, but acts of the kingdom will affect the world. Faced with the world's great needs, it is easy for us to become discouraged and think we cannot make a difference. We may ask such questions as, 'What use is helping a few poor people, compared with the desperate poverty of the whole of Africa?' For my friends helping AIDS orphans and other HIV sufferers in Southern Africa, what is the point of helping a few, when larger numbers are still contracting HIV? What is encouraging a few women not to have an abortion, compared with the growing numbers of abortions? What is the point of helping a drug addict, when you know that even more are becoming addicted?

This teaching about the kingdom down-to-earth shows us that we should not worry about the limitations of our own contributions. We can undertake acts of kindness; we can sow a seed; we can add yeast to the dough. God will ensure that the whole loaf is leavened, and that the small seed grows into a tree.

Even what we often call 'revival', where the power of the gospel affects the whole of society, requires us to have this perspective. In a very interesting recently published book, *Invading Secular Space*, Martin Robinson and Dwight Smith assert that the numbers of people affected by the revivals associated with Wesley and Whitefield were not as great as is popularly imagined. They refer to the fact that fully thirty-five years after the first outbreak of revival, the total membership of Methodist churches was only 30,000.[22] This does not represent the kind of widespread growth that is sometimes imagined by evangelicals today. And interestingly, that number is very small compared with the subsequent growth of Methodism over the next thirty-five to forty years.

In other words, seeds had been planted in large numbers as thousands attended the evangelistic open air meetings, but it actually took time for true growth to take place. Robinson and Smith go on to point out that in the subsequent years there were many other fruits from the seed sown in the Wesleyan revival. Some of the historic denominations were gradually renewed; remarkable social engagement was pioneered by William Wilberforce and the Clapham Sect; the modern missionary movement was born. John Wesley was concerned not only for the salvation of souls, but also for the transformation of lives, as is clear from the wide scope of his writings.

The effect of this kingdom perspective was seen in subsequent generations, so that in the Victorian era, according to the social historian Gertrude Himmelfarb:

Crime and illegitimacy (reliable indicators of wider social and moral attitudes) fell, not merely proportionately, but absolutely, during the period from the 1840s to 1901. The graphs in her book show figures proportionate to population, and these indicate sharp falls on both counts. However, when the population figures for 1841 and 1901 (26.85 million and 41.6 million, respectively) are taken into account, then a small reduction even in the absolute figures can be deduced – a quite astonishing fact.[23]

Encouragement

Secondly, This understating of the kingdom saves us from being disappointed, discouraged and therefore prone to give up, when things do not go as well as we expected in the short-term, or when the 'promises' we have heard are not yet fulfilled. There will be amongst some an emotional response; there will be those who seem keen but then pull back because of preoccupation with the troubles of life. The enemy is active and counterfeit imitations will grow up alongside the genuine article. Even on the macro scale, the takeover of social action initiatives, started amongst Christians, by secular humanism with its tendency towards 'political correctness', can dampen our zeal for this sort of kingdom ministry. Yet Jesus told us it would be like that. The end of the age will show what is of the kingdom. Initiatives today in the UK such as 'Faithworks'[24] are helping Christians to rediscover their confidence in God for the church to be involved in society in co-operation so far as possible with secular authorities, national and local. Secular humanism has not provided the answers, so let us with renewed confidence continue to expect the seed of the kingdom to grow.

Realistic Expectations
Thirdly, it preserves us from unrealistic expectations, yet
enables us to act in faith concerning the purposes of God,
to bring everything in heaven and on earth under the
authority of Christ.[25] On the one hand, some would teach
that eventually Christian government will be set up, will
rule the world in righteousness and prepare a platform
for Christ's return. Others expect things to get worse and
worse until the church is rescued by the 'rapture' from
the time of great tribulation that will come upon the
earth. I believe the biblical teaching is much more subtle
than either of these extremes. Evil will increase, but in the
midst of that, the kingdom will grow in its extent and
effect, but it will not fully be established until Christ's
return. It is only then that all pain will cease, justice will
be fully restored and the nations will be ruled in
righteousness. Yet until that time, we must not be
passive, but must work for righteousness to grow and
affect our nations, and speak out as advocates for the
downtrodden and oppressed. The kingdom may not
come in all its fullness, but we expect his kingdom to
grow and fill the earth. It is an increasing kingdom.

Avoiding Self-Centredness
Fourthly, it preserves us from a self-centred form of the
gospel that concentrates on the individual's personal
salvation and blessing, rather than an obedient response
to the truth of God's kingdom. So often, salvation is
presented in a way which does not represent the full
extent of God's salvation plan to bring his kingdom to the
world: believers are 'saved' by a response to a personal
gospel, but with little idea of the kingdom purposes for
which they are saved.

The criticism can be made, however, that there are ways of

emphasising the work of atonement on Good Friday and Easter which in fact abbreviate the biblical gospel. This happens when the church 'skips over' the earthly ministry of Jesus and focuses on the work of salvation. Western Protestantism is particularly prone to do this, but there is a tendency in all Western theology to separate the cross from the earthly ministry of Jesus . . . The most obvious evidence of this reductionism is the widespread preoccupation with one's individual salvation, effected on the cross, with little attention to the cosmic and communal character of the gospel. As contemporary Western evangelisation continues that individualism, leaving out of its gospel proclamation any sense of the comprehensive and radical good news of God's in-breaking kingdom, it reveals that it is just as human centred as the society it decries.'[26]

Sometimes it seems to me that a gospel is presented which is not much more than an alternative method of self-help, focusing on my personal needs and my personal prosperity rather than my commitment to God's programme in the earth.

Lack of Kingdom Perspective

Is a lack of kingdom perspective in the church a possible reason for some sad facts today? How can it be, for example, that some countries which have the largest problems of HIV/AIDS also have large Christian populations? Could it be that the church has not understood its Christian priorities, and that individual Christians have not been challenged to live a kingdom lifestyle by the grace of God and in the power of the Holy Spirit? How could a country like Rwanda, which experienced revival relatively recently, become known for one of the worst cases of genocide in recent world history? Sometimes it is said amongst evangelicals that if enough of the population were 'born-again', there would be sufficient godly yeast in society to change the culture. Unfortunately, examples such as I have quoted show that this is not necessarily the case. It requires churches with a kingdom perspective, whose view of the kingdom embraces not only personal blessing, but a broad perspective on God's prophetic agenda as revealed in the 'restoration' prophetic scriptures to which I have frequently referred.

Political Involvement

For Christians to influence society and change its culture requires churches to support Christians from amongst them who campaign for justice on the broad scale, who get involved in politics and who offer practical, compassionate care to needy individuals. For example, a church might support both those who are active in seeking to campaign against liberal abortion laws and those who care for single mothers and provide pregnancy counselling services.

Social and political action on the part of Christians requires an understanding of Jesus' way of peace and a gospel of peace to our enemies. Sometimes the exhortation of Jesus to carry the load an extra mile is relegated simply to personal issues of not bearing a grudge or helping our neighbour, or suffering personal loss. However, the context of that teaching was very 'political'; it was a gospel of peace to an oppressive nation. A church that is an agent of the kingdom must understand these implications of the kingdom.

Justice

This 'down-to-earth' understanding of the kingdom must help us look afresh at the issue of justice for the oppressed. Gary Haugen comments that 'As Christians we have learnt much about sharing the love of Christ with people all over the world who have never heard the gospel. We continue to see the salvation message preached in the far corners of the earth and to see indigenous Christian churches vigorously extending Christ's kingdom on every continent. We have learnt how to feed the hungry, heal the sick and shelter the homeless. But there is one thing we haven't learnt to do, even though God's Word repeatedly calls us to the task, we haven't learnt how to rescue the oppressed. For the child held in forced prostitution, for the prisoner illegally detained and tortured, for the widow robbed of her land, for the child sold into slavery, we have almost no vision of how God could use us to bring tangible rescue. It is perhaps more accurate to say that as people committed to the historic faith of Christianity, we have forgotten how to be such a witness of Christ's love, power and justice in the world.'[27]

In Matthew's gospel the kingdom is closely linked with a concept translated 'righteousness' in most of our English versions. The Greek word is *'dikaiosyne'*. As David Bosch points out (his emphasis):

The translation of **'dikaiosyne'** poses problems, however, at least in English. It can refer to **justification** (God's merciful act of declaring us just, thus changing our status and pronouncing us acceptable to him), or to **righteousness** (a pre-eminently religious or spiritual concept; an attribute of God or a spiritual quality that we receive from God), or to **justice** (people's right conduct in relation to their fellow human beings, seeking for them that to which they have a right). Most English New Testament translations reveal a bias towards the second meaning. Often the word **'justice'** does not appear at all in an English New Testament – with important consequences. One discovers this if one translates 'dikaiosyne' in the sayings of Jesus alternatively with 'righteousness' and 'justice'. The fourth beatitude may then refer to those who hunger and thirst after spiritual **righteousness** and **holiness**, or, to those who long to see that **justice** be done to the oppressed. By the same token, the 'persecuted' of Matthew 5:10 may be suffering because of their religious devoutness (**righteousness**), or, because they champion the cause of the marginalised (**justice**).[28]

Bosch goes on to point out that this interpretation has many similar consequences so, for example, it could read that our practice of **justice** has to surpass that of the Pharisees, or that we are to seek God's kingdom and his **justice** before everything else, i.e. not be concerned with our own desires but with the practice of justice for those who are the victims of circumstances and society. We probably should not draw big distinctions in these various meanings. 'Our problem may rather lie in the fact that the English language is unable to embrace the wide scope of "**dikaiosyne**" in one word.'[29]

A 'down to earth' view of the kingdom means that Christians have to stand in a strange position politically. So often issues such as family life and abortion are identified with more conservative or right-wing political parties, whereas a passion for the rights of the oppressed and a society that cares for the poor, are often identified with the more left-wing or social democratic parties. The Christian must not be pigeonholed, but embrace both. Both are aspects of the kingdom. We believe in a missional church, indeed that this is what the church is for, but it must be a church that truly announces the gospel of the kingdom with all the breadth of scope that is set out in the last two chapters if it is truly to have God's intended impact.

Notes

1 Luke 7:36–38
2 Luke 11:37–41; 6:1–5
3 John 6:14,15
4 Matthew 5:41
5 Luke 4:24–29
6 Matthew 13:3,18,19
7 Matthew 13:31
8 Matthew 13:33
9 Matthew 13:44
10 Matthew 13:47,48
11 Acts 1:6
12 Matthew 24:1,2
13 Matthew 21:43
14 Colossians 2:13–15
15 Hebrews 10:1–3
16 Matthew 24:14
17 Matthew 13:10–15
18 Matthew 6:25–27
19 Alpha is described in Nicky Gumbel, *Telling Others* (Kingsway, 1994)
20 Darrell L. Guder, *The Incarnation and the Church's Witness* (Trinity Press, 1999), p. 5
21 Richard Wurmbrand, *In God's Underground* (Hodder & Stoughton, 1968), p. 54
22 Martin Robinson and Dwight Smith, *Invading Secular Space* (Monarch, 2003), p. 67
23 Meic Pearse in *Why the Rest Hates the West* (IVP, 2003) p. 50 quoting G. Himmelfarb, *The De-Moralisation of Society* (London LEA, 1995), II555
24 An initiative of Oasis Trust
25 Ephesians 1:9,10
26 Darrell L. Guder, *The Incarnation and the Church's Witness*, p. 8
27 Gary A. Haugen, *Good News About Injustice* (IVP, 1999), p. 13
28 David J. Bosch, *Transforming Mission*, p. 71
29 Ibid. p. 72

Chapter Seven

Church-Based Kingdom Social Action

We have seen that the Old Testament prophets spoke not only of a future Zion, the people of God, but also of a future kingdom, in which righteousness would reign and good news would be announced to the poor. Just as Jesus was the agent of this future reign of God, the kingdom, when he was here on earth, so the church is the agent of the kingdom now. Each local church is therefore to see itself as a community of people who are the agents of kingdom social action, and such social action projects are to be rooted in and accountable to the local church. As well as the theological reasons we have already considered, there are also, in my view, practical reasons for this model of church-based kingdom social action.

- Though mercy ministries may reach out to all in need without discrimination, it is important that those who are reached and who also wish to become disciples of Jesus are able to establish relationships with Christians, which enable them to be built into the Christian community. We see this in the ministry of Jesus, when many were healed or blessed or fed, but only a few became disciples. Ten lepers were cleansed, for example, but only one returned to Jesus.[1] The ministry of the kingdom through the local church is to bless many, whatever their response, for this reflects the nature of God, who sends his sun upon the righteous and unrighteous and makes his rain fall upon the just and unjust.[2] It is likely that some of those so blessed will turn to Christ, and it is important that they are in a sphere of existing relationships with Christians, where they can then be discipled.

- Clear accountability to local church team leadership brings a vision which incorporates the social action work within an overall vision for a local church, and gives pastoral oversight and guidance both to those committed to the social action work, with all the emotional demands it makes, and to those who come to Christ as a result of this ministry. After we had first set up a house to give full-time residential support to people who had come to Christ from situations of desperate need, I received a phone call one day to tell me that the first resident in whom so much time had been invested had run away. Because it was the first time it had happened, those serving in the house were distraught and the team leader was away on holiday. It was very important for them that their church pastor was able to take time to talk them through the issues and help them understand the importance of allowing space and freedom to someone receiving help. Praise God, that first person who ran away came back, and is now serving God as a missionary in Cambodia.

- Church-based social action enables prayer backing to take place within the local church. Indeed, such projects can be a major focus of a church's prayer life, both corporately and in the cell groups to which those serving in the projects belong. It means the church is praying for people with whom they have real relationships, rather than praying for a separate and somewhat anonymous organisation.

- The church provides its social action projects with a place for recruiting people to the work, in a way that does not conflict with the objectives of their local church.

- Church-based social action enables small initiatives to be taken by church members who feel God has laid something on their heart. It may be that the initiative does not in the end work out, or operates only for a limited period. Because it is within the safety of the ministry of the local church, that is fine; a limited contribution has been made to the work of the kingdom but there has not been the embarrassing scenario of a new organisation set up with great fanfare, only to fold soon afterwards.

- Church-based social action demonstrates to the world what the church is intended to be – a community which not only cares for its own members, but seeks to bless the world in many different ways.

- Church-based social action provides a model which is reproducible in other local churches. We have seen this with some of the social action initiatives taken within our churches in Bedford, which have later been reproduced elsewhere.

- Where there are good relationships with other local churches, it enables people from those churches to join in and then take personal contacts back to their own church for fellowship. In the many social action projects amongst our churches in Bedford, we find that we are providing personnel for one another. For example, people based in other churches in the town who want to work amongst families in need, can work in the project set up in my own church. On the other hand, those from my church who wish to work in pregnancy counselling or a scheme to help those in debt, can get involved in the ministries operated by other churches in the town.

Small Beginnings

When we started our church in Bedford, it was always part of our vision to reach the needy. In those early days we were in contact with a number of people with alcoholic or drug related or occult backgrounds. Quite frequently we took people into our home to live for a few days whilst they were working through particularly distressing issues in their lives. We were quite naïve at that time and I realise that a lot of the burden of care fell upon Scilla because my job was taking me increasingly overseas.

Although it was not funny at the time, we often have a laugh now about one of our early experiences. We had invited some people with particular social problems to spend Christmas with us. Unfortunately, about ten days before Christmas, I was sent on business to the Marshall Islands in the mid Pacific Ocean. I remember it took forty-one hours to get there and then I missed the last plane home via Honolulu and Los Angeles back to London. I therefore had to catch a plane to Guam and then another to Tokyo and then try and get a flight back from Tokyo to bring me back in time for Christmas. I finally made it home late on Christmas Eve. On Christmas morning, I took the Christmas service and then we returned home to lunch. Meanwhile, one of the daughters of the family we were helping had arrived at our house drunk and fallen into a drunken stupor in our downstairs loo. As soon as I had finished Christmas lunch, I went upstairs to our bedroom for something, sat on the bed for a moment and fell fast asleep. Scilla was left to cope alone with the needy family in addition to our young children.

On another occasion we fostered the fourteen-year-old daughter of a woman who had been persuaded to go into a Christian retreat centre for alcoholics in another town. She eventually remained there for over a year. When we first met the family, their electricity and gas had been cut off and the children were reduced to stealing from local shops in order to survive. That period of unexpected fostering was a real challenge, and occasionally a delight. Overall, however, we look back on it as a positive experience.

From Personal to Church-Based

At that time, I became convinced that we needed to start, within the context of the church, a home for people with such difficulties. A couple of years later, Philippa Stroud joined us from her work with Jackie Pullinger-To in Hong Kong, with a similar vision. One summer we were offered a large house to rent by somebody who was not part of the church but sympathetic to what we were doing. This offer came in mid August when most of the eldership team were away! However, because of the vision that we had agreed as a leadership, it seemed so clear that God was in it, that the two of us left took the decision to rent the house as a place to help those who had real social needs. The house was situated in Clarendon Street, Bedford, and thus the 'Clarendon Street Project' was born. Later we planted a church in that part of Bedford, The King's Arms, and this project became part of The King's Arms' work amongst the poor. The history of this project can be read in Philippa's book, *God's Heart for the Poor.*[3]

The initial vision was to see four houses established; a night shelter, a hostel for those who wanted a more permanent place to stay, then a discipleship house, and then a family house to help people reintegrate into society. The King's Arms' work amongst the poor has developed since that time but its basic vision remains the same. The project is integral to the life of the church.

Around the same time, another group in the church was passionate about helping people with severe learning difficulties. Many such people can find it hard to relate to our church services, particularly the level of teaching, but Julie, who led this work, had a passion to see people with such difficulties come to a personal knowledge of Christ and experience the power and presence of the Holy Spirit. Thus was born 'The Acorn Fellowship', which was also part of our church at the time. We then planted a church in the south of Bedford and the Acorn Fellowship ministry became part of that church from its inception. They have seen several saved and baptised, and have regular meetings where those with learning difficulties can experience God and receive Christian teaching at an appropriate level, whilst still being fully integrated as part of a local church in the town.

Having planted out some of our social action projects with the new churches, we felt it important to seek God as to what we should do ourselves. As the Holy Spirit moved amongst us, God began to put upon two of our members a deep passion for families in need. Because of the disjointed patterns of family life today, many people have needs which, in a more stable family situation, would be met by their extended family. We therefore started a project to help bridge that gap and become like an extended family for many in need. We also have kids' clubs serving children and teenagers on our local estates, and we often find now that people are in touch with the church at different levels. Some of the kids come to our clubs, their families are helped through our family ministry, and teenagers are impacted through our youth or schools work, so that in different contexts the whole family experiences something of the kingdom of God and the love of Christ.

Across the World
Obviously my personal experience is firstly here in England, but church-based social action is something that our family of churches is involved with all over the world. Indeed as we plant churches, we encourage each one to have some form of kingdom ministry amongst the needy. In many parts of the world (indeed, I would probably dare to say, in all parts of the world), it is not possible to plant New Testament style churches effectively without this dimension. Here are some examples, from various parts of the world, of the powerful partnership between church planting and kingdom social action.

Pietermaritzburg, South Africa
In 1986, during the apartheid era in South Africa, Pete Dreyer and Brian Andrews, who were then elders of the Pietermaritzburg Christian Fellowship, had a vision of a place where people would enter hopeless and leave equipped. At first their main concern was a massive feeding programme, where thousands of people were fed daily; then in 1992, the old prison in Pietermaritzburg became available to the church, and they founded what is known today as 'Project Gateway'. This operates under the leadership of Pietermaritzburg Christian Fellowship in partnership with other churches in the city, and involves many other local churches in church-based social action in that city.

As part of their individual ministries, a number of city churches lead the different projects that fall under the

Project Gateway umbrella. Their mission statement reflects the original vision, 'To change people's lives by helping them physically, emotionally and spiritually. We aim to uplift people and their community by job and life skills, reaching all people without prejudice, showing the compassion of Jesus Christ and honouring our Creator.' This is a clear statement of kingdom vision. Their projects, which are all led by different churches, include Gateway Christian school, small business training and start-up, a community care project focusing on the effects of HIV/AIDS, a pregnancy crisis centre, an overnight shelter for the homeless, a baby hospice and a women's shelter.

One of the important things to remember in helping the poor is that it is not enough to provide food and clothing, or even training in particular skills. Job skills are no use unless they can be used in an entrepreneurial context. At Project Gateway, they believe that acquiring a job skill alone is not enough to have a significant and ongoing impact in the lives of people trying to make a living in the economic context of South Africa. They therefore aim to empower entrepreneurs with skills that will release them from dependency, and enable them to generate income through the running of sustainable businesses. They do this through finding viable business ideas and then mentoring people personally as entrepreneurs. Gateway itself has acquired considerable expertise in sales and marketing support in order to enable those entrepreneurs to develop their businesses.

Often Christian organisations can help people develop craft skills, for example, but unless there is entrepreneurial skill, then the real causes of the poverty and need are not met. In the kingdom manifesto in Isaiah, the poor move from receiving good news, to experiencing gladness rather than mourning, to being people who rebuild and restore and then have livestock and viable businesses.[4] All this can be achieved through the ministry of the local church and local churches acting together.

Zimbabwe

In Zimbabwe, Brian Oldreive developed a form of agriculture which he felt was more appropriate for African conditions, involving 'zero tillage' instead of the customary deep ploughing of the ground in preparation for sowing. This was then developed through the work of Kingsway Community Church, Bindura, Zimbabwe until in October 2000, the leadership team of Kingsway Community Church sensed a leading from God that they should assist the church in Zimbabwe (especially the rural church) to help their poorest families plant food for themselves. They believe that God gave them that instruction to enable his church to make a prophetic statement ahead of the looming crisis of the national food shortage which, as is well known, came in the end to Zimbabwe. The Evangelical Federation of Zimbabwe was asked to identify ten churches in each province that would need most help with food production, and ten teams were formed, made up of full-time staff of Kingsway Community Church and volunteers from River of Life Church in Harare and Dihlabeng Christian Church in Clarens, South Africa.

Within the space of one month, from the end of November until 21 December, the teams visited over eighty-six churches in all eight rural provinces of the country, with the aim of training approximately thirty families per church in the principles of conservation farming, and giving them seed and fertiliser for planting the moment they received rain. Thus in the span of a month, more than two thousand four hundred families were empowered and enabled to plant food for themselves. This work was supported by churches and other donor organisations in the UK, and the project was named 'Operation Joseph', after the biblical Joseph who preserved a nation in a time of famine.

This was church-based social action on a large scale! And God was at work in it in amazing ways. As one team arrived at one of the churches, an elderly man told them that he had been needing seed and fertiliser but had no money to buy any. That morning, he was able to witness how God provided for him. A man told another team that, because of a death in the family, he had been forced to sell his oxen and had no idea how he was going to plant seed for next year's harvest, now that he had no means to plough. The team then taught that in conservation farming there is no need to plough. People came to Christ, people were healed through the prayer of the teams and people were set free from demonic power – all evidence of the kingdom of God at work.

Kingdom discipleship involves the practical ways in which we live, as well as the spiritual disciplines we learn. Obedience to the training for conservation farming became the single biggest factor (after rainfall) that determined the size of the harvest in these various Zimbabwean villages. The families who obeyed the training and stayed with their weeding programme saw the required result. Where there was high obedience, there were high yields. Where there were low yields this was because of low obedience or, in some cases, because of no rain on time.

Conservation farming uses God-given technology to produce a minimum of 3 tonnes per hectare in the first year; but because the soil improves remarkably when this method of farming is used, the yield can improve to 5 tonnes per hectare from the third or fourth year onward, under average rainfall conditions. This is a wonderful example of how God's kingdom includes caring for the land which provides our food – part of our original creation mandate to till and care.[5] And the local church is to be the agent of the kingdom in this respect, as in others.

Kenya

Edward and Fridah Buria moved to the township of Kambakia on the edge of Meru in 1983. During colonial times, this township had become a place of crime. Hardcore criminals were rounded up from elsewhere and brought to Kambakia, and as well as being a lawless place, it was also extremely poor. Edward and Fridah sensed God saying, 'I want you in this place,' yet all kinds of crime took place outside their home, and their children would sometimes come into the house screaming. Edward and Fridah wondered whether they had made the right decision to bring their family to such a place; one pastor even said to them, 'You have just come to kill your family.' However, through this pastor's influence, Edward and Fridah were the first people to bring a telephone into the village. They became a bit like a police station, because they were reporting all kinds of crime. On one occasion Edward rang the police and received the astonished response, 'Why are you, a pastor, living among the lawless?'

One night they witnessed a gruesome crime, in which a husband chopped off his wife's hand. Edward said to God, 'If this woman dies, I will know you are telling me I have made a mistake and I will take my family and leave. If she lives, it will mean the opposite.' They rushed the woman to the hospital and today, amazingly, she is alive, despite losing her arm and spending three days in a coma. When she came out of the coma, Edward and Fridah knew God was saying, 'Look, I have answered your prayer,' and they began to pray for breakthrough. God said to them, 'This village was given over to evil demons. There is an activity of evil forces operating in the place. I want you to go into every home and speak words of command, cast out evil spirits and ask for my kingdom to come.' They started at about seven o'clock in the evening and for twelve hours through the night they did what God had commanded in home after home. Bringing the kingdom of God involves encounter with evil spirits. Jesus said, '. . . if I drive out demons by the Spirit of God, then the kingdom of God has come upon you.'[6]

The following week, they began to hear about people getting saved. Suddenly the village was engulfed with praise. A church has been planted there now, 'Kambakia Christian Centre', and now has a membership of over two thousand, and from that base one hundred more churches have been planted throughout Kenya. Edward says, 'We praise God for the missionaries who brought the gospel to us. But unfortunately, attached to the presentation of the gospel there was a lot of legalism . . . The vision I have is that in every district of our country, we will see healthy New Testament churches established.' Edward is determined to see grace-filled, Spirit-empowered churches planted, which bring the kingdom of God to their area.

Edward has also been involved in planting churches amongst the Samburu people. During a recent famine in Kenya, the Samburus lost quite a lot of their animals, which are the backbone of their economy. Edward felt God telling him to stand with them and provide goats and cows. At the Stoneleigh Bible Week in the UK an offering was taken to help honour that commitment. He also felt God speaking about piped water. In 2003, water was at last provided to one of the most needy areas. All this was accomplished through the work of a church-planting ministry. In another town, Mbere, alongside the new church plant is a posho mill, where people from the village can bring their maize for grinding. It is creating jobs and income for the people in the church, and at the same time it is serving the community, because previously they would have had to trek many kilometres to have their maize ground.

Just 20 kilometres from the Cape Town to Cairo road (a dirt track in that part of Kenya!), lived the Manyangalo people. Though they had lived on a particular piece of land for several generations, they had no legal documents for its ownership and were in danger of being evicted. One of the elders of the church in Kambakia was an advocate and he took up their case and pursued it right through from the Lower Court to the High Court. Now the Manyangalo have their own land. They were a forgotten people, but now in the name of the Lord, they have found dignity. In place of injustice, the justice of the kingdom of God ('*dikaisyne*') has come through the work of a local church.

In order to support church planting, many businesses have been started. Edward says that God spoke to Fridah and himself through the life of Paul, who was a businessman as well as an apostle. Through his tent-making business, Paul provided not only for his own needs but for those of his whole team.[7] So Edward and Fridah began to enter into agriculture on a small scale, planting maize and beans. They then started a coffee business and although their first farm was destroyed in the drought, the business is still developing and enabling church planting to take place and people to receive income. They now have their own coffee processing plant which is open to other farmers, whom they can charge for processing their coffee. God has also spoken to them about planting trees. They have already planted two thousand, and the vision is to plant one million. The plan is to begin to harvest the trees after three years for timber scaffold poles. This is very simple but is sustainable business; sustainable agriculture, bringing the kingdom of God to the earth.

Russia

A church I am involved with in Armavir, in the North Caucasus region of Russia, has a vision for its church-planting ministry to see the kingdom of God come in many ways. They have established a drug rehabilitation scheme, as have quite a number of churches of different backgrounds within the former Soviet Union. They have a large prison ministry and indeed, see services and almost church plants inside the prisons. They serve Chechen refugees and have an excellent Christian school where Russian and Chechen children are educated together. Although the school has a Christian ethos, it has staff who are not yet believers and children from all sorts of backgrounds, Christian and Muslim and those with no religious beliefs. My wife Scilla has helped with the teaching at the school and has seen the atmosphere of love, joy and peace – the atmosphere of the kingdom of God.

Clarens and Lesotho, South Africa

A few years ago, a burglar alarm salesman from Cape Town, Steve Oliver, took his family on holiday to the highlands region of the Free State near Clarens. On one occasion, during that holiday, they had an opportunity to pray for a village chief who was sick. On their return there a few months later, they found that they were being asked to share the good news in many of the Kraals around. A mighty move of God's Spirit started and Steve, Heather and their family decided to move from Cape Town to plant a church in that area. A church began to meet in the barn on the farm that Steve and Heather purchased. They quickly gathered about eight hundred people, and new churches were then planted in Clarens and across the border to Lesotho.

Steve and Heather discovered that there was no shop in the township near Clarens, so people had to travel to purchase food and were paying a higher price than in the shops in their white suburb. They helped church members to set up a shop not only to serve that community, but also to provide a financial base for the new church, empowering unemployed church members in business skills and creating employment. Then in the fields they began to implement conservation farming. A bit later, because of difficulties and legal disputes, the church across the Lesotho border was forced to leave its building. Some of its members were even threatened with eviction from their homes, but the local community stood up for them and said, 'Don't send these people away, their land produces many more crops.' Recently the World Food Programme has asked the church to take a lead and introduce this farming method (at the World Food Programme's expense) throughout Lesotho. Here, again, is the kingdom of God established through the work of the local church.

Potential Difficulties

In all these examples, we see the powerful impact of church-based social action projects. Nevertheless, it must be admitted that bringing a strong kingdom dimension to a local church can be fraught with difficulties. Social action projects can be resented by those involved in other essential church ministries, because they recruit some of the most enthusiastic people, who thus become unavailable for other church ministries and leadership roles. Sometimes I will hear simultaneously complaints from those involved in projects to the effect that there is insufficient promotion of the project within the life of the church, and from those not involved in the projects to the effect of 'social action is all we hear about, and unless people are involved in this project their ministry goes unrecognised!' Kingdom projects are usually led by dynamic, visionary leaders with plenty of 'get up and go'. They are often the best recruiters of people to the ministry, but not always the best in terms of long-term support of those involved. Furthermore, their vision and passion to reach the poor can make them impatient of their church and its leadership, whom they may regard as lagging behind in terms of the exciting vision. There can be real tensions concerning how fast such projects grow or how expansive they become. This could well be the reason why historically many projects have grown up independently of the life of the local church.

This all requires good leadership which is both visionary and pastoral in its concern. It also requires those with a passion for something to develop patience, and to recognise that building a project solidly requires good foundations in the early stages and careful building thereafter. Sometimes we even have to die to our vision in order to see it raised from the dead. All of Abraham's promises were bound up with Isaac, yet it was Isaac, the fulfilment of the promises, that Abraham was told to sacrifice. His obedience was such that he believed God could raise Isaac from the dead, so convinced was he both of God's promises and of God's command to make the sacrifice. We have to be willing to die to our vision and trust God to resurrect it in his time.

One issue that arises in UK-based projects is whether charitable kingdom activities should be part of the same 'charity' or 'trust' as the local church. On the one hand, this ensures that a project is clearly and identifiably integrated as part of the church community. On the other hand, it can be helpful for the social action project, as it grows, to become legally a separate charity under the governance of its own trustees, but voluntarily accountable to the leadership team in the local church. This can be a wise step both in terms of the legal accountability of the trustees who (in the case of the trustees of the local church) may be somewhat at a distance from the operation of the project and also for reasons of fundraising, which may be easier (though not necessarily so) if the legal organisation is separate.

God has a glorious plan for his church. That plan is to be involved in bringing the benefits of the kingdom and rule of God to those around and across the world. Local church-based social action therefore is one clear way in which we are to fulfil our God-given mandate.

Notes

1 Luke 17:12–19
2 Matthew 5:44,45
3 Philippa Stroud and Christine Leonard, *God's Heart for the Poor* (Kingsway, 1999)
4 Isaiah 61:1–7
5 Genesis 2:15
6 Matthew 12:28
7 Acts 20:34

Chapter Eight

Missional Churches

In the mid 1990s, I read a Church Pastoral Aid Society review of a recent booklet, *Building Missionary Congregations* by Robert Warren, who was at that time National Officer for Evangelism on the General Synod of the Church of England's Board of Mission. The following quote in the review fascinated me.

Halfway through the decade of evangelism [the 1990s were declared a 'decade of evangelism' by the Anglican church], we may have experienced the blessings of Toronto or Willow Creek. We long for growth to take off. We look at our churches and say 'Lord what do you need us to become', these two words are part of the answer: a missionary congregation. When you see it, it's so obvious. Much of the Church of England's way of working derives from 400 years ago when most people were regular members. No-one setting up a church today would saddle it with the structures, buildings and hierarchies which we have inherited. And that's the point, in a Christian age we needed a pastoral church. In the largely pagan age of today, we need a missionary church and that is profoundly different. What does a missionary congregation look like? No-one knows. Are there any in Britain? Possibly not. A missionary congregation is not a pastoral one with evangelistic activities bolted on. It is more radical than that.[1]

While the review was obviously referring to the Anglican Church, I am sure it would have been equally true of non-conformist and even new churches, that their life and church structure were based on a pastoral rather than a missionary model. In the book itself, Robert Warren defined pastoral and missionary churches as follows:

At the heart of the distinction that is being made in this paper between a pastoral and missionary church, is the difference between a church organised around sustaining and developing and promoting its own life, and a church organised around participating in God's mission in the world.[2]

I wonder whether it would still be the case that there are possibly no missionary congregations in England? I think that since the mid-nineties, the growth of 'cells' (evangelistically focused small groups within churches), the proliferation of Alpha courses and, hopefully, a greater emphasis on equipping people for their work in the world as well as within the church, may be changing the culture of church life.

Reaching Local Prostitutes and Unreached Tribes

For example, one church I know on the south coast of England is affecting the community by reaching out to prostitutes on the streets of that town. A special suite of rooms is available on the church premises on the edge of the 'red light' district as a place where the outreach team can bring women back for a drink and further conversation. Many come and end up pouring out their hearts.

Most are very happy to be prayed for and talk further about their need for God in their lives.

While that is a specialist ministry, this church regularly sees people saved in its Sunday meetings and gives major support to overseas ministry, including supporting 'Jimmy', who is the only person saved from his whole people group in Africa; he is being sponsored by the church to translate the Scriptures into his language through Wycliffe Bible Translators. The church also supports through teaching, training and practical help for a new apostolic church-planting movement in northern Uganda. Certainly a missional church at home and overseas.

The World is Our Mission Field

You will notice that the CPAS review, when referring to a missionary church, was not thinking primarily of the sending of people to other nations, but to the fact that a post-Christian culture, like that existing in Britain and most of the rest of Europe at present, requires a missionary church to witness to it.

I recently listened to Bryan Knell of Global Connections, talking about the need to change global mission culture in the UK church. He said that there were two approaches to promoting global mission. The first, and more traditional approach, was to mobilise individual Christians for global mission. The second – and this really is what this book is about – was to challenge churches to get involved in global mission. One of the important points he made was that in order to create churches with a mission culture, it is essential to take the radical step of breaking down the home/mission field barrier from the congregation's thinking. We need to move away from the notion that evangelism is what a few enthusiasts do in the local church at home, and mission is what a few specially called and trained people do as they are sent to other nations of the world. Bryan suggested that we veto all 'home/field' terminology and avoid the word 'missionary' – amen to that! I find myself becoming intensely irritated when I attend conferences where participants are constantly talking about 'on the field' as if that were somewhere else. If John Wesley could say the world was his parish, the twenty-first century church in all nations must say, 'The world is our mission field.' We have a mission field at home – wherever we are – and we also have a mission field into other nations.

Changing Church Culture

In order to become a missionary church, the local church needs to really understand Acts 1:8. Jesus said, '. . . you will be my witnesses in Jerusalem, and in all Judea and Samaria, and to the ends of the earth.' As we saw in an earlier chapter, for the purposes of today's missionary-minded churches, Jerusalem is our home town, Judea is the region surrounding our town, Samaria represents those close to us geographically, but different culturally, and indeed against whom we may have a prejudice, and the ends of earth represents the nations of the world, particularly those who have never yet heard the gospel. I am totally committed to reaching the totally unreached people groups, and spend a lot of my time in that ministry; at the same time, it is important to recognise that in much of western Europe, the evangelical church is totally marginalised and regarded as a sect. This means that most west Europeans have never had an opportunity to hear a clear presentation of the good news of Jesus Christ, nor have they witnessed the power of a community where Christ is loved.

It takes a long time to change the culture of an existing church. It is possible to start the culture of a new church plant on the basis of genuinely being a missionary church, but even then, as it grows and becomes established, there is a temptation to revert to a pastoral model. It is important to keep on teaching and, as leaders, to keep on reminding ourselves, that the essence of the church is that it is a community on mission.

Fellowship and Mission

In what seems a very 'pastoral' letter, the apostle John starts his first epistle with a reminder of this essential nature of Christian fellowship. We can wrongly think of Christianity as rules to be kept, rituals to be undertaken, or even just doctrines to be believed. Whilst it is true that Christian doctrine is very important, as are the means of grace represented by baptism and the Lord's Supper, the way John describes Christianity in this letter is as a 'shared fellowship which is proclaimed to others'. That is the essence of the Christian faith.

John uses the Greek word *'koinonia'*, a much stronger word than the present day English word 'fellowship', which is only used in religious or certain academic circles. When John speaks of *'koinonia'*, he is describing the close and intimate relationship that the original apostles had with Jesus; they spent time in his company, they touched him and heard him and listened to him, they observed the wonder of his relationship with his Father. John then says, 'We proclaim to you what we have seen and heard, so that you also may have fellowship with us. And our fellowship is with the Father and with his Son, Jesus Christ.'[3] The word 'proclaim' is one of the usual New Testament words for 'evangelise'. John is here describing evangelism as a passing on of *'koinonia'* – a sharing with others of the 'fellowship' Jesus shared with the first apostles, with the result that those who hear the message have fellowship with the apostles and therefore together have fellowship with the Father and the Son.

In other words, Christianity is a fellowship, a relationship with God and with each other that is proclaimed to the world. Properly understood, these relationships never become static or inward-looking, because they are by nature always being extended to include others. The words of 1 John 1, quoted above, ought to be a description of every local church. Becoming a Christian is not just about individuals repenting and believing God has saved them so that they will go to heaven when they die (though that is an important part of it), it is about individuals being brought into fellowship ('*koinonia*') with God and with his people. John Stott puts it this way:

> This statement of the apostolic objectives in the proclamation of the gospel, namely a human fellowship arising spontaneously from a Divine fellowship, is a rebuke to much of our modern evangelism and church life. We cannot be content with an evangelism which does not lead to the drawing of converts into the church, nor with a church life whose principle of cohesion is a superficial social camaraderie instead of a spiritual fellowship with the Father and His Son, Jesus Christ.[4]

Again, therefore, we see that the apostle John, in this epistle, defines the church as a community on mission, which is the whole theme of this book.

Cell Life in Missional Churches

Many local churches have found it helpful to develop a form of cell life, which is intended to nurture a sense of being a community on mission. We are still working through the process in my own local church, but our hope is that each cell in our church will become an evangelistic community, and therefore the church as a whole will be an evangelistic community. Whether one adopts a cell church model or not, in order to be truly biblical we must see our churches become evangelistic communities, and evangelistic communities which also have an outlook on the whole world following the pattern of Acts 1:8.

When I was teaching our first 'pilot group' of cell leaders, I tried to place our potential new cell groups into the context of mission. I invited them to imagine that we as a 'pilot group' were suddenly transported to an unreached tribe in Papua New Guinea. What would be the point of our existence there? Surely it would be to reach that pagan culture. Everything we did together would have the objective of reaching the people of that culture. We would seek to befriend them, learn their language, learn their culture, understand how they 'tick', and gradually share with them the gospel of Jesus Christ and demonstrate our community life together as disciples of Jesus Christ to that pagan culture.

Well, without having to be transported to the other side of the world, we are in exactly that situation. We are a Christian community together, called to reach out to the pagan culture around us. In doing that, we obviously still need to worship together, care for one another, support one another, study the Bible together to build ourselves up and correct one another when necessary. We even need to organise ourselves and administer our work, but it is all with the objective of reaching the culture to which we have been sent. It should follow, then, that if we as a group have not been sent to any other culture, we are to reach the people of our own town. Some amongst our group may then be sent to another culture either close to us or in another part of the world. We would still see that as our community reaching the world.

Teaching and Training

For mission to the ends of the earth, it is important to create a church that fosters mission in all sorts of contexts. It is important that the preaching brings vision for mission both nationally and internationally. As we saw in an earlier chapter, men and women should not be thought of as 'missionaries' when they are sent out from the church to another nation, but rather should be 'missionaries' already serving and evangelising as members of their local church. Some will then find themselves working out in fellowship with that local church how a call to another nation can be implemented.

Training in a local church context is an important part of mission. If we are to engage in pioneer church planting in another nation, then this will almost certainly involve starting a small group and then multiplying it. Training for our eventual call should therefore involve starting and multiplying an evangelistically-minded small group in our home church. Why should we expect to have the skills to do that in another culture, if we cannot do it in our own? Just occasionally there are rare people who are so gifted cross-culturally they can be more effective in another culture than at home, but still the heart to evangelise must be there.

I remember a couple coming to see Scilla and me because they had something important to share with us. When they arrived they told us they had reached the final stages of being selected to work for an evangelistic missionary organisation which functioned worldwide, though they were to be involved in the UK. I was their pastor, yet they had not told me until that moment that they had made any such application, nor had I been asked for a reference! They seemed confident that our church would support them financially because of this tremendous opportunity to be involved in evangelistic mission. I asked them about their evangelistic lifestyle in our own town, because I had not really observed it, and to be honest, it was precious little; but they were convinced that once they had joined this organisation then evangelism would be their job and they would become effective evangelistically. I told them that we did indeed want to put money into evangelism – but by appointing somebody to serve full-time in our church as an evangelist (which we did, a short while thereafter). Furthermore, I had to tell them that I did not believe that they would miraculously become evangelistic as soon as they joined this particular organisation; they were unfortunately quite offended by this.

Some will go to serve a particular local church in another nation in a 'helps' capacity, for example in medical or other social action work. It is important that they, too, are clearly serving at home before they go; otherwise, how can we commend them with integrity? Similarly, in terms of church leadership, it is important to be trained for leadership in your home base church before trying to exercise leadership in another nation. I recognise that cross-cultural skills need to be added, but the basic principles of pastoral care and leadership are the same whatever the culture. We have sent a number of people from our church in leadership positions to other churches, to new church plants in this country, and to other nations. To equip them for leadership elsewhere, we make sure that such leaders come regularly to our elders' meetings and function in a leadership capacity in our own church. A friend of mine, who leads a church plant in Central Asia, told me that one of the real bonuses of his recent long leave back in the UK was to be involved in the elders' meetings and discussions of his sending church.

Changing Addictive Behaviour

A few years ago, one of our church members came to see me. A one-time alcoholic, he had found freedom from his addiction through the work of Alcoholics Anonymous, where he had encountered God but had not come to know him personally through Jesus Christ. His wife had then become a believer in Jesus through our Alpha course, so he attended Alpha for himself, became a believer and joined the church. He told me that Alcoholics Anonymous had originally been inspired by Christians but had subsequently become more secular. He wanted to set up such a group on a Christian basis again, within the context of the local church. The idea was to have an Alcoholics Anonymous meeting in the church building and at the end of the evening offer prayer in the name of Jesus to all who wished to stay behind to receive it. Interestingly, he said that his cell leaders were committed to this project and would be willing to oversee it and view it as part of the outreach of that cell group. This is what happened, and the result was truly a community in mission within the context of the local church, dedicated to reaching people with alcohol and other abuse problems; the ministry started within the context of a cell group of a local church. A considerable number of people have been baptised and become part of the church as a result of that ministry; it has now multiplied and changed its format, but retains the sense of being a community in mission within the local church.

Business Development

This pattern is not only effective in this nation. Another of our church members had a passion to support our related church in Ghana by helping develop small businesses there. He had recently retired as Managing Director of a small engineering company in Bedford and wanted to use his skills in church planting mission overseas. As a result, a number of businesses have been set up within the context of the church in Accra led by John Kpikpi, and some of the church plants from Accra and other parts of Ghana are supported by these small business initiatives. A number of people from different churches in Bedford have become involved, offering their expertise in particular sectors of small industry. There is now a bee-keeping project, a water company supplying water to the surrounding district from a borehole sunk on the land belonging to the church, various other agricultural projects and a carpentry workshop; most of the projects have been helped by people from churches in Bedford serving a church in Ghana – truly church-based mission.

Home-Based Support and Accountability

My own ministry is now largely international in character, overseeing church planting in the 10/40 window and supporting leaders of churches in Russia and Ukraine. The fact that Scilla and I are based in a local church enables us to have prayer and personal support. We share with the other leaders some of the important decisions regarding the amount of time we spend in various aspects of our ministry together. We are able to retain good accountability, and I regularly meet with two of our team for open sharing of some of the more personal aspects of my life, including potential temptations and character weaknesses. Scilla and I are now spending longer periods of time in other nations and again, the input of our leadership team has been vital in enabling this to take place.

Another couple who are church members with us have taken on a particular responsibility to support social action projects in churches that I am involved in overseeing. They have helped start drug rehabilitation projects in Tver and Nizhni Novgorod in Russia and have taken work teams to Russia. This creates even greater support within the local church for my ministry and helps to ensure that it does not become detached as a separate international ministry. The teams that they lead are short-term teams, made up of church members using their holidays to serve the churches in Russia. However, I believe that short-term teams help create a desire for longer term mission in the hearts of either those going, or those who hear about what is happening.

In church-based mission, the authority structures need to be clear. If people go to help existing churches in other nations using their skills in social action projects such as medical work or teaching, it is important that they genuinely submit to the local leadership in the church to which they are going whether they are serving 'long-term' or 'short-term'. Sometimes it is assumed that pastoral oversight will still come from the sending church. Whilst a sending church has responsibility to pray, support and possibly help financially, it is important that pastoral oversight of the work lies with the local church in the country concerned. Otherwise there is an undermining of spiritual authority and an unintentional assumption of a neo-colonial attitude to ministry overseas. This applies in both long-term and short-term work. We are very happy, for example, to encourage and support those from Bedford in the work they are doing in Ghana; however, the authority for the work in Ghana comes from the eldership of the church in Accra.

The Kingdom and Work
As the agent of the kingdom, most of the local church's responsibilities for mission and social action are worked out by the members of that church in their everyday

lives. This is something which we, as pastors, must communicate clearly in our teaching about mission and the kingdom. As those serving in the world, whether in secular work or study or at home with our children, we need a sense of commission to the world. All of us are sent out into the world, not just those going out in so-called full-time Christian service! Jesus even sends us out with a 'business' attitude. While it may not sound very complimentary when Jesus tells us to be as shrewd as snakes,[5] he is not despising snakes, but rather saying that just as a businessmen shrewdly looks for any opportunity for business, so we should look shrewdly for any opportunity to extend the kingdom.

As we consider our role as agents of the kingdom within the world of everyday work, we need to understand that work itself is good. Work is not the result of the Fall, but predates it: 'The LORD God took the man and put him in the Garden of Eden to work it and take care of it.'[6] One of the important things to do as we plant churches in areas of high unemployment or under-employment, is to seek to bring people the dignity of work, along with the Christian community.

Being satisfied in our work is a part of God's plan for our lives, and is to demonstrate kingdom values to this world. 'A man can do nothing better than to eat and drink and find satisfaction in his work. This too, I see, is from the hand of God, for without him, who can eat or find enjoyment? To the man who pleases him, God gives wisdom, knowledge and happiness, but to the sinner he gives the task of gathering and storing up wealth to hand it over to the one who pleases God.'[7] Work may be meaningless when God is not in it. In fact, study, pleasure, laughter, big projects, knowledge and the developing of skills are all meaningless unless we are doing it for our Creator, in order to extend his kingdom.

Job satisfaction means not only taking a job suited to my God-given talents, but also being satisfied in God as I perform my job. If money and pleasure are my sole objectives, then my work is, according to the book of Ecclesiastes, actually meaningless. A kingdom value which we take as a missionary people to the world is that though job satisfaction is very important and we will try and help people find it where we can, true satisfaction is found only in God, in acceptance of his will and in working for his kingdom, however adverse the circumstances.

Copying Out Lists

I remember that from the time I started my secular work after I left school, I was determined to find satisfaction in it and do it to the best of my ability. My first job was in the Department of Transport, Abnormal Loads Section. Yes, it does exist, and is responsible for providing hauliers with routes for loads which are too high, too wide or too heavy for normal roads. When I arrived to start work, they were not really ready for me and so I was given the unexciting task of indexing all the routes that had been prepared. I was determined to obtain job satisfaction from copying out those lists! At least it enabled me to learn what the routes were, and within a short time I was performing the more challenging job of providing hauliers with the routes they needed. When I left that section, my boss commended me for the fact that I had now produced more routes than anybody else, even though I was originally only given the job of writing them all into an index. I know many are not happy in their job; however, it is possible to be happy in God in your job, whilst working for creative change when you can. Contentment is an inner quality not dependent on circumstances.

Kingdom people are not lazy at work. They see work

as part of their mission to the world. The book of Proverbs contains much wisdom for us in terms of implementing the kingdom of God at work. 'Go to the ant, you sluggard; consider its ways and be wise! . . . How long will you lie there, you sluggard? When will you get up from your sleep? A little sleep, a little slumber, a little folding of the hands to rest – and poverty will come on you like a bandit and scarcity like an armed man.' 'The sluggard says, "There is a lion in the road"'.[8] In other words the lazy person will make up any excuse to avoid work!

Dignity and Responsibility

As we have already seen, work creates dignity. God worked for six days and rested on the seventh. Jesus said the Father is still working (see Jn. 5:17). Jesus himself worked, and part of our dignity as people created in the image of God is to work hard. Work trains us in responsibility. One of the social conditions often reported in the media today is the 'perpetual student' attitude amongst those in their twenties and early thirties, who shirk taking on responsibility until a later stage in life. In some respects, people reach adulthood earlier today, particularly in terms of physical development and sexual initiation; but in other respects true adulthood, in terms of taking on responsibility, comes much later. Christian young people extend the kingdom by demonstrating that they are willing to take on responsibility.

This is one reason why I feel it is important for most people to be successful in secular employment before they undertake any full-time ministry, whether as full-time pastors in a local church or being sent to other nations in cross-cultural mission. Indeed, one of the qualifications for eldership is that 'He must also have a good reputation with outsiders'.[9]

Profession Not Obsession

While work is important, a kingdom perspective also teaches us that work is not everything. Bill Hybels has said that work is to be our profession, not our obsession.[10] It is a kingdom value to have boundaries and if necessary, to speak to our employers if our work is in danger of encroaching too much on our family life or preventing us from being a meaningful part of the church community, though that community will need to recognise that for some their main calling is to work for the kingdom in their job and therefore prayerfully and caringly support them in that calling. Workaholism is not the same as working hard, but is an inner compulsion based on insecurity. It is usually driven not by greed, or even by power motivation, but by a sense of insecurity and a need to be accepted and valued.

The way in which we go about our daily work is an aspect of the Christian community demonstrating the kingdom. This can be seen in Scripture when Paul addresses the Christian community on this very issue. Even to slaves, who had no choice about their work or their employer, he says '. . . obey your earthly masters in everything; and do it, not only when their eye is on you and to win their favour, but with sincerity of heart and reverence for the Lord. Whatever you do, work at it with all your heart, as working for the Lord, not for men, since you know that you will receive an inheritance from the Lord as a reward. It is the Lord Christ you are serving.'[11]

If it is difficult at work, if the boss is unreasonable or your colleagues scheme against you, by all means stand up against it; there is no virtue in being a doormat! But remember that even if you can do nothing to ease the particular pressures you face, you are still working for the Lord and there is always an eternal perspective to what you do. '. . . you will receive an inheritance from the Lord'.

Justice and Mercy at Work

It is important for Christians to stand up for justice in the world of work and ensure, so far as we can, that advantage is not taken of the weak in terms of power. I served as the chairman of a joint negotiating committee of four trade unions in my place of work for a while, when I worked for a particular government department. I originally became active in trade unionism to defeat a proposal for a 'closed shop' within our workplace. This is a situation that may sound unlikely today, but was a real issue in the 1970s. However, once I got involved in trade union work, I found that I respected the motives of a number of those who appeared to be left-wing militants, and whom I had previously opposed. They, in turn, were grateful for my leadership, which enabled them to express their passion for justice in meaningful ways.

Even in terms of our motives for work, the Bible has some interesting twists. Obviously we will work to please God, to fulfil our God-given dignity and to provide for our families; but we also work in order to be generous to the needy. 'He who has been stealing must steal no longer, but must work, doing something useful with his own hands, *that he may have something to share with those in need*' (my emphasis).[12]

A completed task particularly promotes dignity. Jesus said, 'It is finished',[13] 'I have [completed] the work you gave me to do',[14] and Paul could similarly say, 'I have finished the race'.[15] As kingdom people in the world, we are to persevere until we have finished and not just keep giving up and trying one thing after another. We look forward to God saying 'Well done', and this includes kingdom work done in our secular jobs, not just our service within the sphere of the church. Whether it is in the work place or the home, and whatever it is that we are called to do, perseverance can be built which helps our Christian walk and kingdom attitude.

Integrity and Truth at Work

Work is also an opportunity for the demonstration of personal integrity. It is important to be honest and not steal, or fiddle, or tell 'white' lies. I remember once being told by a colleague that a particular expense was a legitimate claim. Subsequently I found out that it was not, so I went to see my boss to confess and offer to repay the expenses I'd wrongly claimed. He thought I was crazy, but the incident built respect. We also need to stand up for truth when the company is breaking the law or cutting corners ethically. Our basic ethical guideline must be that God is to be obeyed, rather than people. It is important to stand against practices which would harm others, for example, the frequent practice of large firms delaying payment to smaller companies until the last possible moment, often resulting in financial difficulties for the smaller company while the larger corporation gains extra interest by keeping the money on deposit for as long as possible.

We also need to deal honestly with issues by confronting the people concerned, rather than moaning behind the scenes or grumbling and gossiping; workplaces can be full of backbiting. Joseph was even tested concerning his sexual integrity in his workplace. How we relate to our colleagues, how we walk clear of inappropriate behaviour sexually is important for both Christian men and women. There is often a very narrow line between the friendly and the flirtatious. Christian women in the workplace need to deal with unwelcome male attention with firmness even if it risks rejection and has other unfortunate consequences. It is part of the kingdom mission of the church to demonstrate integrity.

Peace Makers and Managers

A Christian is to be a peacemaker in the work environment, not stirring up trouble, though prepared to make a stand for justice. It is important that we deal with conflict and anger in a godly way. We can be righteously angry at injustice or incompetence by those who should know better, but the Bible gives clear steps for constructive conflict management. Anger screws us up inside; repressing our anger damages us, and an explosion of anger damages others. The biblical method of personal confrontation as set out in Matthew 18 applies within the workplace as well as within the church, as does the scripture, 'A gentle answer turns away wrath, but a harsh word stirs up anger'.[16] Matthew 18 provides for firm loving personal confrontation with a view to winning not criticising the offending party but also makes it clear that the way forward recommended there avoids tale-telling and exposure of others faults unnecessarily.

A Christian in a position of management is to demonstrate kingdom leadership. In contrast with many worldly leadership styles, the Christian leader is to serve those under him or her by helping them to reach maximum effectiveness. When Rehoboam succeeded his father Solomon as king, the elder statesmen of Israel advised him, 'If you will be kind to these people and please them . . . they will always be your servants'. Sadly, Rehoboam ignored this wise advice in favour of manipulation, control and exploitation, which led to a rebellion that split his kingdom in two.[17] Lee Brase wrote, 'I have discovered that if you train a man he will become what you are, but if you serve him, the sky is the limit to what he can become. When I learned this it freed me to serve men who have greater capacity than I have.'[18] It is important that the church recognises that our workplaces are our mission field, not only in direct witnessing, though that is important, but where, as a people, we demonstrate kingdom values.

Building Truly Missional Communities

So let's build missional churches: churches which demonstrate an outward looking fellowship; churches with the nations on their heart; and churches where every member sees their job in the world as part of God's mission 'to bring all things in heaven and on earth together under one head, even Christ' (Eph. 1:10). This requires church leaders to teach about church and kingdom, to raise the dignity of the kingdom work in the world and to look at everything in the church programme to analyse how outward focused it is. If, for example, our small groups are merely 'pastoral huddles', our youth work is only to protect our teenagers from the influence of the world, rather than equipping them practically to reach their peers, if our children's work only cares for and educates children of believers rather than involving them in 'kids clubs' to interact with children of unbelievers, then we need step by step to educate the congregation and change our strategy.

Notes

1 CPAS Review, 1998
2 Robert Warren, *Building Missionary Congregations* (Church House Publishing, 1995), p. 4
3 1 John 1:3
4 John Stott, *Epistles of John* (IVP, 1964), p. 64
5 Matthew 10:16
6 Genesis 2:15
7 Ecclesiastes 2:24–26
8 Proverbs 6:6, 9–11 and 26:13
9 1 Timothy 3:7
10 Bill Hybels, *Faith in the Real World*, p. 78
11 Colossians 3:22–24

12 Ephesians 4:28
13 John 19:30
14 John 17:4
15 2 Timothy 4:7
16 Proverbs 15:1
17 2 Chronicles 10
18 Lee Brase quoted in Myron Rush, *Management: A Biblical Approach* (Victor Books, 1983), p. 13

Chapter Nine

The Purpose of the Church – One New Man in Christ

The theme of this book has been that the church exists for mission to the whole world and to advance God's kingdom. In order to fully understand the purpose of the church, however, we shall now look at scriptures which define it more specifically.

In Ephesians 3:10,11 we read that God's purpose, 'was that now, through the church, the manifold wisdom of God should be made known to the rulers and authorities in the heavenly realms, according to his eternal purpose which he accomplished in Christ Jesus our Lord.' In other words, spiritual beings – the angels on the one hand and the dark demonic forces on the other – will be able to see demonstrated before their eyes the manifold (literally 'multi-coloured') wisdom of God and be compelled to admit how wise God is. How is this to come about? *Through the church*. This means that not only is the church to demonstrate the kingdom to the visible world around us, it is also to demonstrate a vital aspect of God's character to the spiritual forces that lie behind this world.

How is the Church to Do This?

To answer this question, we need to look at the context surrounding this verse. In Ephesians 3, Paul is talking about a 'mystery' which was hidden from the writers of the Old Testament, but had now been revealed by the Holy Spirit to the apostles and prophets of Paul's day.[1] What is this fresh revelation that was kept hidden before? It is not the truth that the nations are to be blessed, for that is clearly declared in the Old Testament, even though it seemed to have been forgotten by many of the Jewish people. No, the mystery Paul speaks of is that not only will the nations be blessed, but that Jewish and non-Jewish people groups will be united as one people, one body. '. . . through the gospel the Gentiles [non-Jews] are [made] heirs together with Israel, members together of one body, and sharers together in the promise in Christ Jesus.'[2] In other words, those who were previously divided become one through the gospel.

Hostility Smashed by the Cross

To gain a broader perspective on this statement, we need to look at chapter 2 of the same book, where Paul refers to the 'dividing wall of hostility'[3] which has been destroyed through the work of Christ on the cross. What is the 'dividing wall'? To understand this, we have to envisage the temple as it existed in Jerusalem at the time of Christ. John Stott describes it as follows:

> The temple building itself was constructed on an elevated platform. Round it was the Court of the Priests. East of this was the Court of Israel, and further east the Court of the Women. These 3 courts – for the priests, the laymen and the laywomen of Israel respectively – were all on the same elevation as the temple itself. From this level one descended 5 steps to a walled platform and then on the other side of the

wall 14 more steps to another wall, behind which was the Outer Court, or Court of the Gentiles. This was a spacious court running right round the temple and its inner courts. From any part of it the Gentiles could look up and view the temple, but were not allowed to approach it. They were cut off from it by the surrounding wall, which was a one and half metre stone barricade, on which were displayed at intervals warning notices in Greek and Latin. They read, in effect, not 'Trespassers will be prosecuted', but 'Trespassers will be executed'.[4]

John Stott goes on to refer to the Greek text of one of these notices, discovered in 1871, exhibited in a museum in Istanbul, which reads: 'No foreigner may enter within the barrier and enclosure around the temple. Anyone who is caught doing so will have himself to blame for his ensuing death.'[5]

In other words, this wall represented the barrier between Israel and other nations. God had called Israel to be his people in order for them to be a blessing to the nations, but this had been distorted by Jewish tradition into prejudice against the nations. Paul is arguing that through the cross, Jesus destroyed not the physical dividing wall of the temple, but the spiritual barrier of hostility, prejudice and alienation between Jew and Gentile, in order to create 'one new man' in Christ.[6] As one new nation with one new identity, a unified body of Christ was to represent the fruits of the gospel, free of any barriers between nations. In other words, two barriers, not one, were destroyed when Christ died: the barrier between God and humanity, as represented by the curtain in the temple, was ripped apart[7] so that all who believe in Christ can freely and confidently enter the presence of God; and the division between Jew and Gentile, symbolised by the dividing wall, was also abolished.

Paul goes on to develop this teaching in the remainder of Ephesians 2. He says that the non-Jewish nations are no longer outsiders, but part of one people, one new family or household of God; they are being built together from their diverse backgrounds into a new temple, not like the old temple built of stone, which spoke a message of division and separation, but a new spiritual temple built on the foundation of the apostles and prophets to whom was entrusted the message of the grace of God for the whole world.[8]

Reconciliation Between Races and Classes

In other letters, Paul makes it clear that this reconciliation does not only apply to Jew and non-Jew, but to all such differences of race, class and status which exist between people as a result of the Fall. He says that in Christ there is not only 'no Greek or Jew, circumcised or uncircumcised' but also no 'barbarian, Scythian, slave or free'.[9] The term 'barbarian' was used of nations despised by the Greeks and Romans, probably because of their inability to speak Greek or Latin, while 'Scythian' referred to people groups from the Caucasus region, who were partly feared and partly mocked and despised. There is no room for these distinctions and prejudices in the church, where 'Christ is all, and is in all.'[10]

Another great divider of people is language. Scripture tells us that there was once one common human language, until the episode of the tower of Babel, when men set out to build a tower to reach to heaven, thus seeking to repeat the sin of Adam and Eve, who wanted to be as God. Part of God's judgement on them was to confuse and divide their language, so that they no longer understood each other.[11] In Acts 2, however, we see the first sign of this curse being undone through Christ. When the Holy Spirit came down on the day of Pentecost, people of many different languages heard and understood the believers declaring 'the wonders of God' (v. 11) as the Holy Spirit enabled them. As the believers spoke in the native tongues of their multilingual audience, the curse of alienation between people groups speaking mutually incomprehensible languages was shown to be neither permanent nor final.

If all human divisions are indeed abolished through the cross, then it is important that the mission-minded local church should seek to demonstrate this principle of 'one new man in Christ'. (The phrase 'One new man' refers, of course, to all believers, male and female.) No other power has been able to achieve such unity between people. Throughout history, one empire after another has brought nations into submission, and made an outward show of unity between subjugated peoples. Yet as soon as those empires have fallen (as they inevitably have), the hostilities between the people groups have re-emerged, stronger than ever. We can see recent examples in the break up of Yugoslavia and the former Soviet Union.

International Reconciliation

Though I believe that we should support the efforts of international bodies such as United Nations to bring peace between people groups, it is evident that the humanistic endeavour which such efforts represent is unable to bring lasting peace and forgiveness.

Sometimes, as a result, I believe, of the church's influence, successful steps are taken towards reconciliation. One example of this is the Reconciliation and Truth Commission set up in South Africa under the chairmanship of Archbishop Desmond Tutu. Another is the International Justice Mission, formed in 1994 by Gary Haugen, bringing together of a number of his Christian friends and colleagues. He writes: 'This organisation makes available a corps of Christian public justice professionals . . . to serve global Christian workers when they encounter cases of abuse or oppression in their communities.'[12] Such initiatives are one way of seeking to work out this principle of bringing justice and reconciliation between nations. However, it is also important for the church's mission to include a commitment to demonstrating the truth of 'one new man in Christ' through a community living together as the body of Christ, in which racial, linguistic and historical barriers have no negative effect on their relationships together.

Homogeneous Churches?

A number of missiologists[13] have observed that church growth often happens more quickly within homogeneous groups than among groups more mixed in nature, and have promoted the idea of focusing evangelism on one particular type of people with the result that churches planted are also from one primary sociological or racial group. It is one thing to make the observation, but quite another to make it a matter of church mission policy! I hesitate to disagree with such eminent missiologists, who have a strong desire to see the conversion of many from across all the nations, but I believe that to promote this as a policy undermines part of the purpose of the church on the earth. I also believe that it could adversely affect the genuine extension of God's kingdom which, as we have seen, is not only about winning individual converts, but about building kingdom communities.

John Kpikpi from Ghana addresses this issue in his excellent book on the Christian response to tribalism. Writing about the times of spiritual blindness among the people of Israel, as recorded in the Old Testament, when they adopted horrific practices from the nations around them, he comments on a parallel situation in the church today and says that 'One such horror that we seem to be able to live with quite comfortably is tribalism – the idea that one's own tribe is superior to all other tribes. Widespread discrimination, injustice, division and wars have resulted from the sinful belief which has taken root in people's minds. Furthermore, the exalting of our tribal identities prevents us from fully embracing God's way of life which he has clearly revealed to us in his son, Jesus Christ, and in his written word.' He goes on to say that:

Our continent of Africa is seeing what is probably one of the highest rates of conversion to Christianity in our world today but very little seems to change with respect to the living conditions of our peoples. So although we know that God, through his word and Spirit, is the one who builds great and prosperous peoples, we do not seem to be seeing anything of that nature occurring. Might it not be the case that the barriers set up by tribalism and wrong cultural practices have essentially kept God's word at bay, preventing him from invading, and so transforming, our culture at its heart?[14]

Darrell Guder puts it this way:

The homogeneous principle of evangelism and church growth is rooted in very understandable psychological and social realities. We like to be with people who are, on the whole, like us. We would like our Christian friends, the fellow members of our churches, to be more or less like us as well. When we expand this process, we see it at work in culturally exclusive forms of Christian witness and church formation. The result has been the pollution of Christian witness with racism, classism and ethnocentrism. The process at the levels of both personal experience and corporate culture encounter may be psychologically and sociologically understandable. But it stands in complete contradiction to the witness we are taught to practice by Jesus.[15]

Jesus himself seems to have deliberately cut across cultural barriers. In his prototype church, as we have noted earlier, he combined a tax collector, who would have been regarded as a quisling for Rome, with a zealot – a revolutionary against the Roman yoke.[16] He touched lepers, talked to women, healed the children of Gentiles and allowed prostitutes to touch him. He went to parties with all sorts of unsavoury characters. He was demonstrating what Paul would later teach: that in Christ all these differences are abolished.

Reaching Multi-Ethnic Cities

This has huge implications both for our missions strategy to other nations and also for our attempts to reach our multicultural cities which are, in that respect, very much like the cities of New Testament times, in which Jews and Gentiles of many nationalities lived and worked side by side. At the beginning of the twenty-first century, our similarly multi-ethnic communities provide wonderful opportunities for this aspect of the kingdom and church's mission.

In my own local church, the multicultural nature of my home town of Bedford has provoked us to seek to be a church which reflects those many different cultures. Some towns and cities have become increasingly multi-ethnic recently because of growing numbers of asylum seekers and economic migrants. Many university towns have increasing numbers of overseas students. There are tremendous opportunities now to reach the nations 'on our doorstep'.

There are also people of different cultures who have

lived amongst us for thirty or forty years, sometimes without learning English or integrating very much into English society. Second or third generation members of these people groups may seem to have been assimilated into English culture but often function differently in relation to family ties and marriage. Children brought up in other cultures, for example, the children of missionaries, are described as 'third culture' kids because they do not fully belong to either their 'home' culture or the culture of where they live. We do not always take cognisance of the fact, however, that we have many such 'third culture kids' living in the UK, the children of immigrant parents who have only partially adapted to western culture. Many Asian Christians (and those of other faiths), for example, fear for the future of their children, who are growing up in the secular, sexually permissive atmosphere of today's humanistic Britain.

Being Strategic

We need to recognise that different strategies are needed to reach different types of people. For example, asylum seekers are often fairly open to new friendships and the gospel because, having come to this country out of dissatisfaction with political, religious or economic conditions where they lived before, they are already open to change and new relationships. For example, a church in the north-east of England has recently seen between fifty to a hundred Iranian asylum seekers come to faith and regularly attend their church services.

There has also recently been a second wave of migrants coming to Britain as people came in the 1950s, to take on jobs in the Health Service and other public sector areas where there are once again shortages of workers. We started an Alpha course in a home amongst such recently arrived people and saw several saved.

In contrast to the openness of many recent migrants to the UK, those groups of people from other religious backgrounds who have settled here long-term, have remained within their own ethnic communities, which they are seeking to preserve against the 'threat' of western culture with which, sadly, they often identify Christianity. Such people can be as difficult to reach here as they would be in their former country, except that there are no laws in this country against religious conversion, as there would be in some Muslim states. To reach these groups, we therefore need strategies similar to those we would employ in Muslim countries; i.e. long-term friendship building, faith and much prayer; prayer for breakthrough, prayer for the sick, prayer that these people may have dreams and visions of Jesus.

Another group is students and language learners, who, like other newcomers and temporary residents, are often very open to friendship and new ideas, have inquiring minds and are not necessarily prejudiced against Christianity.

Caring for Strangers

There has always been a strong biblical emphasis on offering kindness and caring hospitality to guests, including 'aliens and strangers', and I am sure that God's heart has not changed in this respect! The people of Israel were commanded, 'When an alien lives . . . in your land, do not ill-treat him. The alien living with you must be treated as one of your native-born. Love him as yourself, for you were aliens in Egypt. I am the LORD your God.'[17]

In terms of economics, they were told, 'Do not go over your vineyard a second time or pick up the grapes that have fallen. Leave them for the poor and the alien.'[18] There is also a solemn warning: 'Cursed is the man who withholds justice from the alien, the fatherless or the widow.'[19]

The scattering of people groups was common in biblical times, and was used for the fulfilment of God's purposes: Abraham moved in obedience from Ur to Haran and then to the land of Canaan;[20] the people of Israel were refugees in Egypt, then moved out en masse to Canaan; Jesus himself was a refugee in Egypt;[21] Priscilla and Aquila had to move when Jews were ordered to leave Rome.[22]

Questions We Face

These truths have raised important questions for us in our own church and I'm sure many others have found the same. These are questions we all need to think through, both theologically and practically, if we are living in multi-ethnic areas

- Do we believe in 'multi-cultural church', multi-ethnic church or churches where one culture or ethnic group predominates?
- How do we demonstrate 'one new man in Christ' in practice?
- How many languages can we serve in one church/ service?
- Should we have separate congregations serving different ethnic groups within one church?
- Should we have separate cell groups for different people groups?
- How do we relate to churches of one people group, such as Afro-Caribbean, Nigerian, or Ghanaian churches?

We have found that it is important to move on several fronts at once, to have different strategies for different peoples, whilst always trying to express 'one new man in Christ'. So in Bedford we relate very well to a Punjabi-speaking church in town where we give a measure of oversight and care, and yet we also have had Punjabi translation in our own services, using headphones. Similarly, some of our cells have operated in up to four languages, others just in one language, such as Punjabi. One of the important challenges we are facing is to create a multi-ethnic leadership team. The New Testament church in Antioch, which became a great missionary base for many years, had a multi-ethnic leadership team. Obviously we must not compromise the qualifications for eldership, but we may have to take definite steps towards bringing people of different cultures on in their ministry and responsibility, in order to demonstrate what we believe God is calling us to be.

Practical Hints

We need to develop local church strategies specifically to reach those of other nations in our neighbourhood. This must be accompanied by teaching, prayer and 'seed sowing'. In our own church we taught on the subject of a multi-ethnic church and our belief that the composition of our church should reflect the town in which we live. We set up an Asian outreach team to work full-time for a number of years, reaching a particular area of our town. In fact, most of the Asians now coming to our church are not directly the fruit of that! However, I believe that the principle of 'as we sow, so we reap'[23] applies to this sort of work, so we sometimes sow in one place but reap in another.

The teaching of English enables us to get into the homes of people of different ethnic groups; we have found that offering to teach children English has been a step towards building friendships with their parents. Other churches I know have set up language schools specifically to show Christian kindness to refugees and others coming to this country.

We need to develop courses that are appropriate for

different people groups. Alpha works well amongst those of certain backgrounds, but it is not always helpful for Muslims as it starts with the question 'Who is Jesus?' There are better courses for reaching Muslims which start with the Old Testament historical background to the coming of Christ, and show how Jesus fulfilled the story. One example is a course called 'All the prophets have spoken'.[24] We have found it helpful to have Third World evangelists ministering amongst us; for example, we have held evangelistic meetings with Ram Babu, a gifted healing evangelist from India.

Friendship and welcome are important. When one Asian couple started to come to our church, they were invited into the home of one of our elders. They commented that though they had been in England for nearly thirty years, this was the first time they had had a meal together in a white English home!

Developing Cultural Understanding

There are of course many other issues to be faced, which we are perhaps better trained and prepared for when being sent to another country with the gospel, but are not so aware of when people come to our nation from another. Cultural issues surrounding marriage are an example. It has been one of our conditions for many years that if a couple are to get married in our church, they must first go through our marriage preparation course. However, this is less suitable in the case of semi-arranged marriages, where it is considered inappropriate for the couple to spend a lot of time together before their wedding day. We are therefore having to find ways of doing marriage preparation after the marriage! The biblical position regarding marriage is that it should be in the Lord.[25] There is no specific guidance as to how that marriage should come about in a particular culture. Our method of courtship is a western cultural practice rather than a Christian freedom though, of course, forced or unwilling marriages are obviously wrong.

Another western cultural practice that has been challenged is our assumption that children go to bed at a particular time in the evening and the parents then come to cell group. Those from some cultural backgrounds normally take their children with them, and so we have created intergenerational cells without intending to! We have also found that the large weddings and engagement ceremonies we attend are tremendous opportunities to share the Christian faith.

With asylum seekers, there are of course legal issues to be aware of. It is important that we stand up for people who are now part of our community and help them obtain justice, yet we must also be careful to be strictly honest. I know of one asylum seeker who did not tell the truth on his original application for asylum in this country. When he became a Christian he realised his dishonesty was wrong, and therefore decided on appeal to change his story. His lawyer considered this tantamount to inviting the failure of his application. The judge, however, recognised the man's integrity and understood that, having become a Christian, he would be subject to persecution in his own nation if he returned. He was granted leave to stay!

Multilingual Worship

This truth of 'one new man in Christ' is vital, wherever we go with the gospel. Many of the churches with which I am associated in South Africa have been working hard to ensure that they have multi-racial services and that the worship reflects the different ethnic groups present and indeed becomes distinctively 'African'. It is wonderful to be in a Sunday morning service and hear songs, prayers and prophecies in Afrikaans, English and Zulu in one meeting. One of my friends from Bedford, who has gone out to be involved in church planting in Africa, is a songwriter and worship leader. Within a year of being there he has written songs in Zulu as well as his native tongue.

I have referred earlier in this book to Steve and Heather and their work in Clarens and Lesotho. At first, they had two congregations in Clarens, one English-speaking and one Sesoto-speaking, but they have recently integrated the two. This integration has been brought in at cell level as well, so that wealthy whites are now attending cell groups in some of the kraals of the Basuto people. This is in an area of South Africa that in apartheid times was noted for its strong right-wing attitudes.

Prophetic Anticipation

All these examples are given to help us find creative ways of fulfilling God's purpose for his church to demonstrate his manifold wisdom to the principalities and powers. It is also a prophetic anticipation of the great day to come when all nations worship God together before his throne.[26] I firmly believe that the church today must express as far as possible our hope for the future. This is part of what it means to be an eschatological people, a people of the last days, a people who live in the light of God's future purposes. When we see people of different nations worshipping together now, we are demonstrating to the world what we eventually will be as a result of the gospel triumphing amongst every people group.

Notes

1 Ephesians 3:5
2 Ephesians 3:6
3 Ephesians 2:14
4 John Stott, *The Message of Ephesians* (IVP, 1979), p. 91
5 Quoted by John Stott, see above, p. 92
6 See Ephesians 2:15
7 Matthew 27:51
8 Ephesians 2:19–22
9 Colossians 3:11
10 Colossians 3:11
11 Genesis 11:1–9
12 Gary A. Haugen, *Good News About Injustice*, p. 16
13 See for example the writings of Donald McGavran and C. Peter Wagner
14 John Kpikpi, *God's New Tribe* (Accra, Ghana: Hill City Publishing Ltd.), pp. 6,7
15 Darrell L. Guder, *The Incarnation and the Church's Witness*, p. 48
16 Matthew 10:2–4
17 Leviticus 19:33,34
18 Leviticus 19:10
19 Deuteronomy 27:19
20 Genesis 11:31; 12:1
21 Matthew 2:14,15
22 Acts 18:2
23 See Galatians 6:7
24 Yehia Sa'a, *All the Prophets Have Spoken*, (Good Seed International, 2001)
25 See 1 Corinthians 7:39
26 Revelation 5:9

Chapter Ten

Culture and Contextualisation

As we engage in world mission which is church-based and which involves church-planting strategy, we need to be aware of what is appropriate in the culture that we are aiming to reach with the gospel, and to plant churches which reflect local culture and so can effectively reach people of that culture. This principle is known as 'incarnational mission' or 'contextualisation', and stands in contrast to the many instances in the past of western Christians unhelpfully exporting their own culture along with the gospel – 'everything from harmoniums to archdeacons', as Lesslie Newbigin so colourfully expressed it![1]

In this chapter, we will look briefly at the issue of culture in order to understand certain basic principles that we need to have in our minds. This short chapter could in no way claim to be an exhaustive or definitive consideration of this issue, and there are many books written on this subject which I would commend for further study.[2]

John Stott put it very well:

> The overriding reason why we should take other people's culture seriously is that God has taken ours seriously. God is the supreme communicator. And His Word has come to us in an extremely particularised form. Whether spoken or written, it was addressed to particular people in particular cultures using the particular thought-forms, syntax, and vocabulary with which they were familiar.[3]

Serving Other Cultures

The gospel truths are unchanging, but we can adapt as servants to each culture in order to reach each culture, as Paul did: 'Though I am free and belong to no man, I make myself a slave to everyone, to win as many as possible. To the Jews I became like a Jew, to win the Jews. To those under the law I became like one under the law . . . so as to win those under the law. To those not having the law I became like one not having the law . . . so as to win those not having the law. To the weak I became weak, to win the weak. I have become all things to all men so that by all possible means I might save some. I do this for the sake of the gospel, that I may share in its blessings.'[4] It is important to notice Paul's use of the word 'slave'. This means that I am willing to serve another culture, without holding onto my own rights or even my own freedom, if that freedom were to stop me serving other cultural contexts.

It has been said that Paul released the gospel from its Jewish clothes in order to reach the Gentiles of his day, and Martin Luther released the gospel from its Latin clothes in order to make the gospel clear to the ordinary person in sixteenth-century Europe. What is happening today and what is needed today, is the release of the gospel from its distinctively western clothes, in order to allow every culture to access it freely.[5]

Three Elements in Culture

As we consider what goes to make up a culture, we should bear in mind that every culture contains three different kinds of elements.

- Firstly, there are things that make a particular culture open to the gospel. Every culture contains elements of tradition and practice which are not in conflict with the gospel and which can be used to bring the gospel home to people.
- Secondly, there are neutral elements which can be used to the glory of God, which illustrate the variety and richness of his creation and which, when redeemed, demonstrate his multi-coloured wisdom. These include music and art, hospitality, attitudes to time and many other things.
- Thirdly, there are negative elements in every culture which hinder or oppose the spread of the gospel. These are strongholds which must be demolished. In my book, *Demolishing Strongholds*, I explain this in much more detail and give examples of these three categories.[6]

Oral Learning

We also need to bear in mind that different cultures have different ways of learning and communicating. Western culture has for a thousand years relied heavily upon the written word and a logical-sequential, conceptual way of thinking, whose origins date back to the ancient Greeks. In other words, we are a literate rather than an oral culture, and we think in logical and abstract ways. Many other cultures (and, of course, a significant proportion of people in our own culture) rely much more upon spoken, or oral, methods and a more concrete, visual or kinaes-thetic approach. Concrete learners will understand and interpret stories and examples more easily than they will understand an abstract concept; visual learners will learn from pictures, diagrams and models more easily than from verbal descriptions and explanations; kinaesthetic learners will learn by doing something practical, rather than by listening or reading. So in order to engage effectively with another culture, we need to be aware of what are its dominant communication and learning methods. Even within our own culture, people learn in all these different ways, and effective teachers and communicators will draw on all of them as appropriate.

I personally enjoy teaching cross-culturally. I even enjoy teaching through interpretation, strange as that may seem, because it enables me to develop a different sort of rhythm, and brings home to me the importance of being very clear about what I am saying in the face of the constant reminder that I am speaking to people of a different culture. When I am teaching in more orally based cultures, I always use lots of stories, and quite often I act them out spontaneously, perhaps getting willing (and sometimes rather unwilling!) people from the congregation to join with me.

Many of those we are seeking to reach with the gospel are 'concrete thinkers', rather than 'conceptual thinkers'. We have examples of both categories in Scripture. For example, Paul and Jesus were making the same point when Paul said, '. . . my God will meet all your needs according to his glorious riches in Christ Jesus',[7] while Jesus said, 'Look at the birds of the air; they do not sow or reap or store away in barns, and yet your heavenly Father feeds them. Are you not much more valuable than they? Who of you by worrying can add a single hour to his life?'[8] Both scriptures are teaching us to put our trust in God for our material provision. One is expressed in conceptual language and the other in concrete language.

Both are valid ways of teaching today, as then, and for 'concrete' thinkers, stories are very important. Even some of our 'conceptual' theological terms, such as redemption and justification, were originally 'concrete', everyday words used in the slave market or the law courts, but when they become detached from their origins by the passage of time or by a change in culture, their impact can be lost on concrete thinkers.[9]

Today, at least half of the world's population receives most of its information orally, rather than by the written word. So as we seek to plant churches in other cultures, we must train those leading the churches to teach in ways that are appropriate to oral communicators. This is something that I often emphasise as I travel around church plants in the Muslim world and run training workshops for people serving there.

Many oral communicators can read, but do not easily comprehend or use the information read. Rather they need to hear it in an appropriate oral format in order to understand and use it. 'Being an oral communicator has nothing to do with intelligence levels. It is simply the preferred learning style of probably a majority of the world.' (See reference note 10, below.) Jesus used oral communication. In his language of Aramaic, his words were poetry which was easily memorised by the masses. He also taught for kinaesthetic learners too. He trained his disciples to *do* what he did rather than simply listen to him and take notes! Most missionaries are highly literate. And we who learn in a literate manner lose the ability to receive and process information orally. In a book on reaching Muslim women, an experienced missionary makes the following point: 'My friend Fatima has memorised the phone numbers of all her friends. In contrast, I have trouble remembering my own phone number! Fatima can read a recipe but can't follow the instructions without seeing someone else make the dish. Once she has seen it made, she can make it repeatedly without mistakes. I need to read the recipe every time I make the dish.'[10] An excellent example of kinaesthetic learning.

Chronological Bible Storying

The truths of the Christian faith have come down to us in the written form of Scripture, so it is perhaps understandable that as we try to raise up indigenous leadership in a new church, we tend to look for a highly literate person from the culture to train, so that they can teach the same truths in their own language. However, literate communicators are not always effective at communicating orally.

One method that has been developed for both evangelism and disciple-making among those with oral communication skills is 'chronological Bible storying'. It is significant that both Paul and Stephen presented a chronological overview of the Old Testament as they were sharing the gospel,[11] as did Jesus when talking to his friends on the Emmaus road.[12] Clearly, the telling of the story is a vital element in the communication process. Futhermore, oral and literate communicators tend to find different truths in the same story. For example, in the Old Testament story of Joseph, oral communicators tend to focus on forgiveness, the importance of family unity and the fact that God interprets dreams. Those with a more literate approach tend to focus on the moral issues, the sovereignty of God, and the fulfilment of Joseph's vision. However, both are valid collections of truths to be learnt from the story of Joseph, and oral and literate communicators can therefore help and complement each other's learning.

Use of Jesus' Parables

The parables in the gospels are very powerful in this context. Indeed they make much more sense to those living in cultures closer to that of Jesus, than they often do to westerners. This is illustrated later in this chapter in the case of the parable of the prodigal son. A book that is helpful in giving the true meaning of the parables is *Poet and Peasant and Through Peasant Eyes* by Kenneth E. Bailey.[13]

Churches to Reflect Culture

When we plant local churches, it is very important that they reflect the culture of their own people group, otherwise the gospel will be seen as something foreign or western. In many societies, there are enough genuine barriers for people to overcome in order to become followers of Jesus, without us erecting unnecessary additional ones. I enjoy being in our African churches where the style of worship and dance reflect the African culture. I remember going to one church in Uganda. The worship was first led by a western-style band, singing western songs. There was then a break for the offering and for the children to go to their classes. After the break an African band took over using only drums and then the worship really started!

In many cultures, it is more appropriate to sit on the floor than on chairs. I have noticed, however, that sometimes chairs are provided for the wealthy and for westerners. We must be careful in this context not to transgress the teaching of James, which speaks more directly to that situation than to western mega-churches with plush seats for all! 'My brothers, as believers in our glorious Lord Jesus Christ, don't show favouritism. Suppose a man comes into your meeting wearing a gold ring and fine clothes, and a poor man in shabby clothes also comes in. If you show special attention to the man wearing fine clothes and say, "Here's a good seat for you," but say to the poor man, "You stand there," or "Sit on the floor by my feet," have you not discriminated among yourselves and become judges with evil thoughts?'[14] When I have visited such third world churches, I have found it very difficult to teach sitting on the floor, because I like to walk around a lot as I speak; however, I have made the adjustment! In the west, we stand up to preach, though I notice that in Luke 4, Jesus sat down to preach.[15]

Thinking Biblically About Culture

There are many other examples that I could give of ways in which we can promote the gospel by being aware of what is culturally helpful and appropriate. When we consider the subject of prayer, we find in Scripture that there are examples of people kneeling in prayer, standing in prayer and prostrate in prayer, so the way in which we pray can easily fit in with local cultural understanding.

However, we must be careful that we do not make biblical precedents into biblical commands, or build new religious traditions under the guise of being culturally aware! It is important that we do not countenance any form of legalism under the guise of respecting local culture. For example, in many eastern cultures, I would not put my Bible on the floor if I was speaking in an evangelistic context or where a weaker brother was present, because someone from a Muslim or Sikh background would consider that I was disparaging a 'holy book' and what it stands for, and take offence. At the same time, however, I have to be careful not to give the impression that it is more 'holy' to do something in a certain way. It is the truth in the Scriptures that is holy, not the paper and ink with which it is printed. I would therefore teach this to the leaders in this context so as to try and prevent a wrong legalistic practice emerging from my genuine desire not to offend.

Musical Styles

We have to be very discerning in some areas; for example, amongst certain people groups, the use of music bands may be frowned upon in a religious context but permitted in a secular cultural context. Similarly, joyful music may be considered appropriate within secular folk music, but not in religious worship. Some have argued that in reaching Muslims we should be very careful not to use joyful songs. One writer puts it as follows: 'Sitting to pray and singing joyful choruses can seem blasphemously flippant to the devout Muslim'.[16] I agree that we have to be careful in an evangelistic context not to alienate people unnecessarily, but we also need to teach the importance of joy in our faith, and enable those who become followers of Jesus to express their joy in appropriate cultural forms, and not be restricted by religious taboos. In some cultures, no kind of singing or music is associated with religion at all. This was a challenge in one of the church plants that I am aware of, where it proved very difficult to introduce singing in the church gatherings. It was not that these people never sang, but that in their culture singing was used entirely in secular contexts and had never been associated with faith.

It is of course important that the music we use reflects the local culture rather than our western style, if possible. Sometimes, we need to pray for a creative local musician to be converted, or even a musicologist to be brought onto the team. However, it is important that we do not delay worshipping because we do not yet have songs to express it in the local culture; I encourage people to feel free to use translations of western songs in the meantime. However, their *objective* must be to have songs written in the local style, and in a style which is contemporary; we must beware of resurrecting 'ethnic' music traditions that are now outdated or irrelevant in that culture.

When I first visited the churches that I am associated with in India, they were singing western songs. Then as churches were planted in other language groups, more culturally appropriate songs began to become popular. One of our church leaders, Virendra Patil, who leads a church in Gujarat, is an example of an excellent musician who has been converted to Christianity. His CDs are now amongst the best-selling Christian CDs in the whole of India.[17] What he manages to achieve is a truly Indian style of song but in a *contemporary* Indian idiom; he has not gone back to a classical form of Indian music used centuries ago! Virendra writes his songs in Hindi, and when I was in India, I noticed with interest that not only were Hindi speakers much freer in their worship using his songs, but even English-speaking Indians worshipped more freely because his songs were in a cultural style that was natural to them, despite the fact that English and not Hindi is their mother tongue.

Counter-Cultural Necessities

However, there are some things in church life that need to be deliberately counter-cultural. Even the style of church leadership may well have to be counter-cultural because few cultures (in the west as elsewhere!) demonstrate servant leadership or genuine team leadership. Although 'team' is not a biblical word, it expresses the New Testament plurality of leadership. In the Old Testament, Moses came down the mountain with the decrees. In the New Testament, when facing a crucial decision, the church leaders made their decision on the basis of 'It seemed good to the Holy Spirit and to *us*'[18] (my emphasis). Team leadership genuinely reflects a New Testament value and therefore has to be imported into cultures where there would naturally tend to be just one dominant leader. In describing leadership in the New Testament, Paul used both the familiar Jewish idea of 'elder' (*presbuteros*) and the secular Greek term of 'overseer' (*episkopos*) so that both Jew and Greek would understand what he was teaching.

Defining Contextualisation

Understanding all these issues is what is meant by contextualisation. This word is defined by different people in different ways. A literal definition is 'Contextualisation concerns itself with how the text of [Scripture] relates to the context of a people group' – Rick Love.[19] Our evangelical view of the inspiration of Scripture implies contextualisation. It was not dictated by God, as is claimed for the Qu'ran or the Book of Mormon. Furthermore, the New Testament was written in '*Koine*', or Greek, the language of the street or marketplace, and not in formal, classical Greek.

Another definition that has been given is that contextualisation is the effort to understand (and to take seriously) the specific context of each human group (and person), both on its own terms and in all of its dimensions, that is, cultural, religious, social, political and economic, and to discern what the gospel is saying to people in that context. Others would describe it as 'Meaningful and appropriate cross-cultural transmission of biblical truth which is faithful to its original intent and sensitive to culture.'

Contextualisation or incarnational mission is a biblical concept. Jesus was incarnated into a first-century Jewish context. Many of the issues faced by the early church were concerned with how far the religious culture of the Jewish Christian could be imposed upon the Gentiles.

Paul's Freedom

Paul was remarkably free from cultural bias in the way he lived and taught. From a legalist's perspective, he could be thought highly inconsistent, but in fact, he was truly working out his philosophy of being like a Jew to the Jews, etc. So, although he told the Galatians that 'neither circumcision nor uncircumcision means anything', yet in a Jewish context he had Timothy circumcised[20] and himself took a Nazirite vow.[21] When approaching the intellectual pagan Greeks, he honoured their religious devotion, even though it was pagan, and in the altar to the unknown god found a point of contact with their culture.[22] He then quoted from two Greek poets to support his teaching,[23] although 'The quotations in their proper pagan contexts express points of view which were undoubtedly quite repugnant to Paul' – N.B. Stonehouse.[24]

> Not only are these quotations from pagan poets but they also refer unequivocally to Zeus, the chief god in the Greek pantheon. And yet Paul uses them to depict the character of the Christian God. Evidently he was prepared to allow their truth, but only if Zeus was recognised as somehow depicting Yahweh; it is obvious that much of what pagans said about Zeus certainly could not be applied to Yahweh. Only where it was in agreement with the Old Testament and Christian revelation in Jesus was Paul prepared to take the steps' – Howard Marshall.[25]

For Paul, then, there were limits to contextualisation. In the process of contextualising the gospel and the church, we, too, must discern where the boundaries are between the legitimate adoption of good or neutral cultural elements, and the wrong adoption of ungodly elements which is likely to result in the gospel being lost or adulterated, and the church lacking clarity and purity. Ungodly strongholds of wrong thinking must still be confronted. The Israelites failed to confront such crunch issues when they adopted the worship of Baal from the cultures around them.

A Biblical Framework

A good example of Paul confronting a cultural issue is his teaching on food offered to idols, where we see him giving wise and discerning advice that avoids being dogmatic, but rather is culturally sensitive, while remaining true to gospel principles. His teaching on this subject comes at some length in 1 Corinthians 10:18–33, 1 Corinthians 8 and Romans 14. The needs of the weak brother, Paul says, are to be taken into consideration, and the 'weak' are defined as those who would be offended by what was eaten at certain feasts. There is clear teaching not to join in pagan festivals, but certain cultural practices seem to be accepted, such as taking the food served at the festivals and sharing it with relatives or friends. The food itself, says Paul, will not hurt us; the real issue is how it looks to others and affects their consciences. Love for one another is what counts, and acceptance of one another with our differences. Paul says Christians are free to eat the food with a good conscience, but if a 'weaker brother' is unhappy with the idea of eating food that has first been offered to an idol, the 'stronger' Christian should not eat it either, for the sake of the weaker brother's conscience. He refuses to be drawn into making detailed, rigid laws which could then be refined into abstruse legalistic practices. Unfortunately, legalism is what many Christians want; even new Christians sometimes prefer to have rules to follow, rather than learn to live by the Spirit. In planting churches cross-culturally, this must be resisted at all costs, and mistakes of the past must not be repeated.

Even in the most appalling pagan contexts from which people were saved, Paul refused to give 'laws' but instead helped people to live under new covenant grace and in the power of the Holy Spirit, and this is what we must do, even in teaching immature believers converted out of pagan contexts or ' Folk Islam'. (Most Muslims live under the power of Folk Islam, which is basically a body of superstitious and animistic beliefs, rather than formal Islam.) Above all, we must teach the grace of God. The letter to Corinth is specifically addressed to immature Christians converted out of a licentious pagan background, yet even in the context of believers continuing to go to temple prostitutes, Paul does not impose a 'law' but uses a new covenant argument and says, 'Don't you know that your body is a temple of the Holy Spirit? How can you take what is a temple of the Holy Spirit and join it to a prostitute?'[26] Roland Allen comments that:

> [Paul] had not been absent from Corinth more than 2½ years when he wrote the first epistle to the Corinthians; yet in spite of the fact that the church had enjoyed the instructions of Apollos and was notorious for the wealth of its spiritual gifts, it is perfectly manifest that fornication was a common offence. How then did St Paul deal with this very serious difficulty? There is not in his letters one word of law; there is no indication that the Jerusalem Council had issued any decree on the subject. There is not a suggestion that he desired a code of rules or a table of penalties. He does not threaten offenders with punishment. He does not say that he will take any steps to procure their correction. He beseeches and exhorts the Lord's people to whom the Holy Spirit has been given to surrender themselves to the guidance of that Holy Spirit, to recognise that He is given to them that they may be holy in body and in soul, and that uncleanness

necessarily involves the rejection of the Holy Spirit and incurs the wrath of God.[27]

All other religions except Christianity tend to be ritualistic and legalistic; they rely on people carrying out prescribed rituals, obeying prescribed rules and depending on good works to make them acceptable to God. The Christian faith is exactly the opposite. Righteousness is given to us as a free gift.[28] We no longer live under law but under grace and in the power of the Spirit.[29] As we live by the Spirit we do not fulfil the desires of the flesh.[30]

I remember teaching on the subject of grace in a particular church in Scandinavia; the pastor said to me afterwards, 'I agree with you theologically, but it is too dangerous to preach it!' I know what he meant; the message of grace can sound like a licence to sin, but it is not. In fact, teaching grace is the only way of producing mature Christians who can live by the Spirit and make godly decisions, and this must be our objective, whatever the culture. However, in teaching grace, we need to take account of the way of thinking of those to whom we are speaking. In my experience, the doctrine of grace has a particularly powerful application when taught, in the Islamic world, although it strikes against a stronghold in Islamic thinking. It is by grace that we know God and are brought into relationship with him and experience his mercy, while in Islam, we can at best know and submit to his will, but cannot know him in a close relationship. Though Allah is the merciful one, there is no assurance that he will be merciful to me.

Grace to Shame-Based Cultures
We also need to learn how to apply the wonderful teaching of God's grace in a way that relates to the motivating factors in that culture. Many cultures, inclu-

ding most Islamic cultures, are 'shame'-based societies. Shame is a very powerful motivator. Often in shame based cultures, the distinction is not so much between what is right and what is wrong, as what is acceptable and what is unacceptable, or shameful. Shame can lead to real bondage. Poor families will get into terrible debt rather than reduce their costs by holding a more modest marriage or circumcision ceremony, which would bring shame on the family. Bringing shame on the family or the village is often what prevents people making a public profession of faith in Christ.

Each fallen culture needs to have a mechanism for bringing controls against the excesses of sin in human personality. Some cultures are primarily guilt based like our western culture, others are shame based, others are anxiety-based. For example, often in animistic cultures in Africa, the control mechanism is fear; fear of offending against ancestors, for example, or an 'almost fanatical faith in the magic of certain symbols . . . thus especially conducive to states of morbid fear and anxiety' – a comment by T.A. Lambo, a Nigerian psychiatrist.[31] Folk Islam similarly has anxiety-based controls.

Shame results from fear of people's anger at any misbehaviour, and the desire for approval (from parents or society at large) is more important than the actual performance of a deed. Loss of 'face' is particularly feared. As a Haitian proverb puts it 'Dirty clothes are washed within the family'. There would be loss of face or shame involved if others knew the particular family problem.

Anxiety, shame and guilt are all seen in the story of the Fall of humanity in the Garden and these are all met by the power of the grace of God. Adam and Eve hid (anxiety), they were naked (shame), and they shifted the blame (guilt).[32] I am told that there are over one hundred and fifty references in the Old Testament to shame and its derivative words. Shamelessness is considered bad in Scripture, 'they do not . . . know how to blush'.[33] Jesus scorned the shame of the cross.[34] The cross was shameful; it was a curse.[35] Therefore we must preach grace through the power of the cross into a shame culture. This means that as western preachers we have to change our methods and illustrations because we are more accustomed to preaching grace in a 'guilt' context.

> Grace offers the support that allows trust to replace anxiety, acceptance to restore honour where we were shamed and forgiveness to resolve guilt. . . . This unconditional love called grace is a gift, gratuitous, unmerited, an acceptance that cannot be earned or achieved. Whether ones theology views grace as 'the appraisal of humans as worthful' or 'the bestowal of worth on humans', the grace is unmerited and the worth unearned. Whether one's theology has stressed the anxiety – punishment – release motif of grace, or the shame – alienation – reconciliation model, or the guilt – condemnation – forgiveness pattern, grace offers acceptance, inclusion, forgiveness as gift.[36]

The Prodigal Son
The parables can be often better understood in a shame context. What the younger son said to his father in the parable of the prodigal was shameful. By asking for his inheritance early, he was in effect saying, 'I wish you were dead.' The father overcame the power of 'shame' first shockingly by agreeing to his sons request but then, upon the prodigal's return, by running to greet his son. This would be unheard of in that sort of culture. It would not be dignified for an older man, particularly a wealthy landowning farmer, to run. Many of the parables help us in presenting the doctrine of grace to shame-based cultures.

Cultural Strongholds

However, as well as seeking to express church life in the forms of a particular culture and as well as learning how to teach the vital doctrine of grace to the various cultures, we must also demolish the strongholds of that culture. What is a stronghold? Ancient fortified cities, as well as having a wall around them, also had a stronghold, a tower inside the city which could be defended by a few soldiers, and within which people in the city could hide from their enemies. Thus it was not enough to conquer a city simply by entering its walls; it was necessary to invade the stronghold as well. An example of this is given in Proverbs where it says, 'A wise man attacks the city of the mighty and pulls down the stronghold in which they trust'.[37]

We use the word 'stronghold' to mean wrong thought patterns and ideas which Satan and his demons influence, behind which they hide, and which can govern or dominate individuals, communities, cultures and nations. As people come to Christ, those strongholds need to be demolished, so that they can no longer give a home to wrong attitudes and demonic influence.

In my book *Demolishing Strongholds*, I tell the story of a particular visit I made to India. I repeat the story here because it so clearly illustrates what a stronghold is. A particular couple asked me to pray for them, because they could not have children. I felt prompted by the Holy Spirit to inquire why they were unable to have children, expecting, from my western perspective, a gynaecological reason. The reply from the wife was that they were unable to have children because she had killed a cobra when she was a teenager. When I inquired further, I discovered that in that particular culture it was not considered appropriate for a girl going through puberty to kill a snake; she should call a man to kill it for her. If she killed the snake herself, she would be unable to have children. I sought to demolish that stronghold of wrong thinking by teaching and prayer. Praise God, when I next returned two years later, the couple showed me one little child and the evidence of another one very much on the way!

Folk Islam

As I travel around the world I find that many have become believers but have not got free from the strongholds that affect their culture. For example, it is estimated that 70 per cent of all Muslims are influenced by Folk Islam. Formal Islam has therefore spread only a thin veneer over animistic beliefs and practices. The fact that people are in bondage to the superstitions of Folk Islam provides an opportunity to demonstrate the power of the name of Jesus, but is also a major challenge to our discipling of people in such contexts.

Bill Musk, in his excellent book on Folk Islam,[38] defines the ten felt needs in popular Islam as: fear of the unknown, fear of evil spirits, powerless before shamanic power, fear of the future, shame and not belonging to the in-group, disequilibrium, sickness, helplessness in crisis, meaningless in life and vulnerability of women. To attempt to meet these needs, such women seek spiritual power through magic and witchcraft, which are essentially manipulative methods of trying to get one's own way or one's own desires fulfilled, whether for the blessing of oneself, one's family or property or fields, or for harm to those who offend us or get in our way. It is important that Christian converts see the difference between this and Christian prayer, which makes our requests known to God with an attitude of submission to his will and faith in his sovereignty and his working all things together for our good.

As Rodney L. Henry points out in his excellent book, *Filipino Spirit World*,[39] when Christianity is brought to a nation, it often happens that the major doctrines of the Trinity, the person of Christ, the cross, heaven and hell and the means of salvation are preached, but strongholds in the culture, such as animistic beliefs, are not addressed. Those saved will thus believe in the 'big' truths of the Christian faith whilst living their everyday lives in bondage to superstition. So it is important that we do not become so enamoured of respecting the culture that we fail to challenge its strongholds in new believers.

Planks and Specks

However, another factor that is important for mission is that it is no good seeking to demolish the obvious (to us) strongholds in another culture if we have not become free of the strongholds in our own culture. That would be like trying to take the speck out of my brother's eye whilst having a plank of wood in my own.[40] It is very important that before engaging in mission into another culture, I receive help to walk free of any strongholds in my own life, resulting from my upbringing or the wrong thinking of my own culture. In the western world-view there is a stronghold of scientific rationalism or modernism. This means that I only accept what I can see and understand; intellect and analysis are exalted above faith, and the spiritual world is either denied or seen as less real than the physical. We often find that people from non-western cultures can be stronger in faith in a powerful, miracle-working God than we are.

There are also strongholds of self-centredness which means that the pursuit of pleasure becomes our greatest goal. Our attitude is 'How does this affect me?' Many today get saved but have a self-centred lifestyle and a consumerist attitude, even towards Christianity and the local church.

Linked with this is the stronghold of individualism. In the west we think individualistically (or at best in the context of a small nuclear family) rather than as a community. This is contrary to the heart of God, because God exists in perfect community: Father, Son and Holy Spirit. He has created us for community and his heart is that believers should express that unity – a corporate witness to the world and a corporate response to Christ. The stronghold of self-fulfilment is thus seen to be idolatrous. We forget that we are here primarily to serve, not to be fulfilled. When I teach on 'strongholds' in a non-western context, I first acknowledge the strongholds that can affect my own culture and find that this gives me greater moral authority to address strongholds in the culture I am reaching.

Contextualisation Not Syncretism

We believe in contextualisation both for the way we explain our gospel message and for the way we build churches which reflect their local culture. However, we must not permit contextualisation to degenerate into syncretism. Syncretism is the attempted reconciliation of diverse or opposite tenets or practices, especially in philosophy or religion. It is an attempt to combine incompatible beliefs, some Christian and some which arise out of the religion or philosophy of the people being reached. We must be very careful in our mission to not allow such syncretism but again, we must watch ourselves because, as the 1978 Willowbank Report states, 'Perhaps the most insidious form of syncretism in the world today is the attempt to mix a privatised gospel of personal forgiveness with a worldly (even demonic) attitude to wealth and power'.[41]

Church-based mission therefore aims to present the gospel in a way that is appropriate to and relevant for those to whom the gospel is presented. This means that we have to re-examine what could be inappropriate teaching methods for a majority of the world's population even though we have become very attached to the methods of western preachers. The goal of church-based mission is to plant new churches in other cultures which reflect that culture and are therefore able to reproduce themselves rapidly in that culture. Such churches must therefore be 'contextualised' without falling into the dangers of syncretism because the desire to be culturally relevant has caused there to be insufficient recognition of the need to pull down the strongholds of wrong or even demonic thinking in that culture.

Notes

1 Lesslie Newbigin, *The Finality of Christ* (SCM Press, 1969), p. 107
2 Some examples: Charles H. Kraft, *Christianity in Culture* (Orbis Books); Phil Parshall, *Muslim Evangelism* (Gabriel Publishing); Rick Love, *Muslims, Magic and the Kingdom of God* (William Carey Library)
3 Cooke and Stott (eds.), *Down to Earth* Studies in Christianity and Culture (Eerdmans, 1980), pp. vii-viii
4 1 Corinthians 9:19–23
5 From an article by Ralph D. Winter in *Mission Frontiers Bulletin*, September–October 1996. Available to download from http://www.missionfrontiers.org/1996/0910/ffmm.htm
6 David Devenish, *Demolishing Strongholds*, pp. 99–124
7 Philippians 4:19
8 Matthew 6:26,27
9 For a much more exhaustive treatment of these differences see Roy Joslin, *Urban Harvest* (Evangelical Press, 1982)
10 'Discipleship of Muslim Background Believers Through Chronological Bible Storying' in Fran Love and Jeleta Eckheart (eds.), *Ministry to Muslim Women* (William Carey Library, 2000)
11 Acts 13:16–41; 7:2–53
12 Luke 24:13–27
13 Kenneth E. Bailey, *Poet and Peasant* and *Through Peasant Eyes* (Paternoster, 1983)

14 James 2:1–4
15 Luke 4:20
16 From an anonymous unpublished paper in a debate on Muslim evangelism
17 Virendra Patil, *Prabhu Tera Pyaar*, *'Yeshu Mere'* (Frontier Publishing and Trading Co. Pvt. Ltd., 3 Pali Darshan, 33rd Road, Bandra (w), Mumbai, 400050
18 Acts 15:28
19 Rick Love, *Muslims, Magic and the Kingdom of God*, p. 10
20 Acts 16:3
21 Acts 21:26
22 Acts 17:23
23 Acts 17:28
24 Quoted in Rick Love, *Muslims Magic and the Kingdom of God*, p. 53
25 Cooke and Stott (eds.), *Down to Earth* Studies in Christianity and Culture p. 26
26 See 1 Corinthians 6:15,19
27 Roland Allen, *Missionary Methods – St Paul's or Ours?*, p. 113
28 Romans 5:17
29 Romans 8:1–9
30 Galatians 5:16
31 T.A. Lambo, *Patterns of Psychiatric Care in Developing African Countries*, p. 444, quoted in David W. Augsburger, *Pastoral Counselling Across Cultures* (John Knox Press, 1986), p. 121
32 Genesis 3:8–13
33 Jeremiah 6:15; 8:12
34 Hebrews 12:2
35 Galatians 3:13
36 David W. Augsburger in *Pastoral Counselling Across Cultures*
37 Proverbs 21:22
38 Bill Musk, *The Unseen Face of Islam* (Monarch Publications, 1989), p. 76
39 Rodney L. Henry, *Filipino Spirit World – A Challenge to the Church* (OMF Literature, 1986)
40 Matthew 7:3–5
41 The Willowbank Report published in *Perspectives on the World Christian Movement* (Pasadena, California: William Carey Library, 1981)

Chapter Eleven

The Dangers and Difficulties of Apostolic Mission

I was listening one day to the pastor of one of the churches for which I have oversight responsibility. He told me how his church had been driven from the building they owned, and he himself had been harangued by an angry crowd at the police station. Because of the intense pressure, he and his family had fled their house for one night. The next day they discussed the whole thing as a family and decided that, despite the threats, they should go back home and trust God.

Later the sixteen-year-old daughter of the family filled in some of the details for me. They had received telephone calls threatening to burn the house down when all the family were in it; on another occasion there was a phone call to say, 'We know which classroom your children are in; we can take them out any time we like.' Then she turned to me with a glow on her face and said that when she remembered all the testimonies of people being miraculously healed in the name of Jesus and many others giving their lives to follow Jesus, it made it all worthwhile. Earlier she had been translating for me as I listened to one of the leaders of the church talk about the miraculous healings and stories of salvation that they had experienced as a result of their regular prayer ministry.

I know that my visits and the prayers of the churches I represent give encouragement to those in difficult situations, and I realised that I was there to encourage a church that knows far greater pressure than I am accustomed to. Because I am based in the west, with only occasional forays into more dangerous parts of the world, I need particular grace and wisdom from God to serve such churches where I have oversight responsibility.

As we have seen earlier, a recovery of apostolic ministry is important today in order to follow the biblical pattern of church-based apostles laying foundations in new churches that are established elsewhere. This is the biblical basis for church-based mission, and one that I am seeking to be involved in developing. It means that we have to think prayerfully about our response to the suffering which, for Christians in many parts of the world, is as intense as it was during the persecutions of New Testament times. Sometimes there is suffering because the government is opposed to people becoming Christians and indeed, there are countries where it is illegal to change one's religion from Islam to Christianity. There are other places where it is constitutionally legal to see people 'change their religion' but where there can still be tremendous opposition from fundamentalists or other militants. In other places there can be violence and pressure from families and the community, even though the country in question may be a secular state in name.

Taking Up the Cross

In his excellent book on missions, *Let the Nations be Glad*, John Piper has a chapter entitled 'The Supremacy of God in Missions Through Suffering'. In it he says:

> To take up a cross and follow Jesus means to join Jesus on the Calvary road with a resolve to suffer and die with Him. The cross is not a burden to bear; it is an instrument of pain and execution. It would be like saying, 'Pick up your electric chair and follow me to the execution room' or 'Pick up this sword and carry it to the place of beheading'. Or 'Take up this rope and carry it to the gallows'.[1]

We have strange ideas in the west of what is meant by 'taking up our cross', and tend to misuse the phrase 'It's a cross I have to bear' to describe anything from an unfair boss to a bad cough, failing eyesight, or even one's mother-in-law! It is true that in whatever culture we live there will be pressures and problems to face, but it is when we are genuinely involved in church-based mission across the world that we face the reality of suffering for Christ's name. And this is what it means to 'take up our cross'; not the pains and annoyances that are simply part of human existence in a fallen world, but the particular kinds of suffering that we face as believers living in an environment that does not yet acknowledge Jesus as Lord.

Following Paul's Example

The New Testament is full of examples of suffering for the gospel's sake. On a number of occasions, Paul catalogues his own personal sufferings,[2] and his letters contain much encouragement to the churches he planted, which were often birthed in circumstances of persecution. As we are involved in mission today, we will find that we, too, have to face situations similar to those that faced Paul and the New Testament churches, so it will be helpful for us to take note of the kinds of issues Paul addresses in his letters.

In his first letter to the Corinthians, Paul was addressing problems of party spirit, division, misunderstanding of spiritual gifts, and the immaturity of people converted directly from a pagan culture, which was resulting in immorality and even drunkenness at the Lord's Supper. As we are engaged in mission, we have to address these issues in grace, as Paul did, and seek to bring new believers to maturity.

When Paul wrote to the church in Galatia, he was passionately concerned that they seemed to be falling away from the doctrines of grace and into bondage to legalism.

What we see here is an example of the pressure on an apostle ministering on the pioneering edge. Indeed, in one account of his sufferings, Paul says that above all his other concerns was the pressure of the care of the churches.[3] Our gospel is preached amidst pressure of all kinds: building the church involves pressure; seeking to develop church-based social action and mission leads to pressure.

Cut Off From the Family

Even as I have been writing this book, I have experienced some totally unexpected pressure and tension. On the very morning that I am now writing this chapter, my wife received a letter from her sister, who is in the Exclusive Brethren. When we left the Exclusive Brethren thirty-four years ago, Scilla was totally cut off by her family. However, a few months ago, we visited her father and for the first time in thirty-four years were invited in to talk to him and her brother and sister. But the letter we received said that we were to call no more and that we would never be allowed in again. This has obviously been very difficult for Scilla, but does enable her to sympathise with people from Muslim cultures who are cut off from their family when they come to Christ. There are pressures, then, in church life and in mission which do not relate to direct persecution.

Persecution of New Churches

In his first letter to the Thessalonians, Paul was writing to a recent church plant, following Timothy reporting to him on its progress.[4] This letter is considered to be one of Paul's most personally revealing letters in terms of his own feelings, and demonstrates the close relationship he had with the churches he planted; he regarded them as family rather than an institution. 'We were gentle among you,' he wrote, 'like a mother caring for her little children. We loved you so much that we were delighted to share with you not only the gospel but our lives as well, because you had become so dear to us.'[5]

It was encouraging to Paul to hear good news of the progress being made in a new church; I, too, always find it encouraging when I hear good news of our new church plants. However, Paul was writing to this church because he had had to leave Thessalonica much earlier than he had intended, because of persecution.[6] He knew that the new believers in that town were experiencing the same persecution and he was desperately concerned to hear whether they were standing firm in the faith.[7]

I also feel that way when getting reports from some of the church plants that I am involved in overseeing. The following quotations are from a prayer letter I received a short while ago, from the wife of one of our team leaders.

Thank you also for praying for 'A' and the situation in her village. It is good that 'A' and her sister keep pressing into God, but the situation in itself is still loaded. Shortly after we left, two men came to their house, dragged her father (a non-believer) out of the house, pulled his trousers down (such shame in that culture) and then beat him up for 4 hours. Lots of other people from the village came and watched, but nobody intervened. The whole family is very frightened and the father is still in pain. 'A' has also lost her job and the verbal persecution seems to have no end ('we'll throw you out of the village, you idol worshippers, you religion sellers,. . .'). From what I can tell, the toughest bit for 'A' is that her non-believing relatives take such a beating. For herself she does genuinely count it an honour to suffer for the name of Jesus. We still want to keep the goal in view (and prayer!) to start a new 'Life Group' there soon. Only God can smooth the way for that to happen.

'B', our babysitter. God is doing miracle after miracle in her. Early on there were all these people she needed to forgive, her mother who didn't want her and then committed suicide when she was only eight months old, her father who rejected her as well, the grandmother who did take her in but has been abusive ever since (saying 'you killed your mother when you cried too much as a baby,. . .') 'B' has told her grandmother that she is a believer and her grandmother has hit the roof. When I went there yesterday, she was spitting fire at me, just about hitting me. Whom she is hitting, lots, is 'B'. She had deep scratches all over her body and said she was really hurting from having been hit all over her body with a bottle. Today, she has just come to our house. The grandmother sent her, to get her name erased from the 'list of Christians in our town'. There is no such list. 'B' hasn't denied Jesus (who keeps showing himself to her in visions and dreams) but she's pretty much at the end of it. Yesterday some aunts came over and they've all been hitting her, bashing her head into the wall until her teeth were bleeding. She's got a black eye as well.

I recall an occasion when we had invited some friends to the Christmas carol service in our home church in Bedford. We asked them back to our house for mulled wine and mince pies afterwards and one of them said to me, 'How can you live with yourself, preaching in places where, if people believe what you preach, they could suffer?' The question was not asked in a confrontational way, but out of a genuine inquiry. The twenty-first century humanistic mind cannot understand the wonder of knowing Jesus and the willingness, therefore, to suffer for his name, and this mindset can be a stronghold even for western believers. Indeed, I was told by a Christian worker who supports the underground church in China that a preacher from America, visiting Hong Kong, said that if the people in the Chinese church really had faith, they would not be suffering in the way they are!

When we talk about restoring the church to New Testament values, we must realise that it will mean much of our ministry being restored to conditions like those of the New Testament. New Testament churches were often planted in circumstances of opposition, suffering and difficulty. This was not so all the time, and suffering is not something we should directly seek! But times free of persecution were unusual enough to be remarked upon: 'Then the church throughout Judea, Galilee and Samaria enjoyed a time of peace. It was strengthened; and encouraged by the Holy Spirit, it grew in numbers, living in the fear of the Lord.'[8]

Standing with the Suffering Church

It is important that we, as Christians, have a sense of solidarity with suffering Christians across the world, even when we ourselves come from situations where there is not much obvious suffering. It is particularly important when we are addressing the subject of mission.

It helps to earth our vision in reality; and the very challenge of suffering is to stimulate faith and encourage the sending of more people to be involved in the battle. For a Holy Spirit-inspired people with a passion for the gospel, understanding the difficulties will motivate us more, not less. In the chapter already referred to, John Piper records the execution of Wycliffe missionary, Chet Bitterman, by a Columbian guerrilla group in 1981. The result of this man's death was to unleash an amazing zeal for the cause of Christ. 'In the year following Chet's death applications for overseas service with Wycliffe Bible Translators doubled. This trend was continued. It is not the kind of missionary mobilisation that any of us would choose but it is God's way.'[9]

We should also remember that although for many of us the devil is not operating through direct persecution, this does not mean he is not working! Indeed materialism, complacency, over-busyness, comfort and ease can stifle the activity of the gospel as much, or even more than persecution. Jesus promised, 'In this world you will have trouble. But take heart! I have overcome the world.'[10] Having an understanding of what the rest of the body of Christ is going through helps us fight the devil's very different tactics in our own culture, as Peter tells us: 'Resist him, standing firm in the faith, because you know that your brothers throughout the world are undergoing the same kind of sufferings.'[11]

The Example of 1 Thessalonians
So Paul's letter to the church in Thessalonica gives us a clear example of how to address these issues as we engage in church-planting mission. It may be helpful to read the first two chapters of 1 Thessalonians at this point and allow the words to impact us and, particularly if we are involved in leadership, to teach us how we, too, can

encourage those going through such difficulties.

Paul refers to his own example; he had had to leave Thessalonica in a rush, as we have already seen, and he had previously left Philippi after being beaten, thrown into prison and suffering indignities inappropriate for a Roman citizen. He then commends the Thessalonian believers for becoming 'imitators of God's churches in Judea' (1 Thes. 2:14) in their endurance of persecution – an example of how one church can provide a good example for another to imitate. We do not expect all churches to be the same outwardly; they will each reflect their own culture. Yet they can all encourage one another and imitate one another in learning how to resist the devil as he brings suffering upon them. Such suffering is supernaturally accompanied by joy; this is the effect of the Holy Spirit's working. In his challenging opening to his letter, James tells us, 'Consider it pure joy, my brothers, whenever you face trials of many kinds'.[12]

Suffering as Part of the Apostolic Foundation

The understanding of suffering is an important part of the apostolic foundation to be laid in new churches. I recall one occasion in an Islamic country, when I had been teaching a number of churches and leaders what that foundation consists of, according to the New Testament. One brother came up to me afterwards and was very appreciative of my teaching; he told me that he realised that in some of the church planting he had been involved with, he had not fully laid apostolic foundations. Then he challenged me with the question, 'But what about suffering? You did not teach us on the importance of suffering as a foundational truth for all believers. We have to teach our new converts how to cope with suffering. Even as they come to faith, they know they may well have to suffer for his name.' I realised my mistake; although I have addressed that subject in certain contexts, I had not previously presented it as an important foundation for church life and for individual discipleship. Yet Paul had taught this to the church in Thessalonica as part of his laying a good foundation. He had taught that suffering was the Christian's destiny. Indeed, one of his reasons for making a return visit to the churches he had founded earlier was to encourage them in the face of suffering, as recorded in Acts 14. He and Barnabas worked to establish the churches more securely by appointing elders, but also by 'strengthening the disciples and encouraging them to remain true to the faith. "We must go through many hardships to enter the kingdom of God," they said.'[13]

It is important, then, that willingness to suffer is taught as part of the foundation for all churches and for each individual's life. Often we preach the benefits of the gospel, as we should, and we rejoice when someone has come to Christ, as we should; but we must not stop there. If a new believer does not understand what it means to take up their cross and follow Jesus, then everything that goes wrong in the future, including opposition from family or authority, will present a threat to their faith.

There is a great danger in converts seeing the Christian faith only in terms of benefit to them. As Dietrich Bonhoeffer put it, 'The cross is not a terrible end to an otherwise God-fearing and happy life, but it meets us at the beginning of our communion with Christ. When Christ calls a man, he bids him come and die'.[14] According to Jesus' teaching in the parable of the sower, inability to endure suffering is one reason why the seed does not come to maturity. Jesus says of the seed that falls on a rocky place, 'When trouble or persecution comes because of the word, he quickly falls away.'[15]

The Grace of God at Work

As well as making sure that we teach this foundational truth, it is important for all involved in mission leadership to have faith in the effectiveness of the grace of God at work in those we have reached. Just as Paul had been hurried out of Philippi, so he had to leave Thessalonica in a rush. It is sometimes said that he was only in Thessalonica for three weeks,[16] and the challenge is raised, 'Surely we can plant a vibrant, evangelistic church in three weeks if Paul did!' However, this is almost certainly a misunderstanding. It is true that he preached in the Jewish synagogue for three weeks, but it seems that he must have been there longer, as there was also time for a mainly Gentile congregation to have been gathered; it says they turned to God from idols,[17] a description unlikely to apply to Jewish converts!

The result was that even though the apostle could not stay in Thessalonica long enough to do the thorough work he ideally wanted to do, there was still a vibrant missionary church planted there. The churches in Thessalonica and Antioch are two of the best New Testament examples of missional churches. The Bible records that the Thessalonians were a model to other believers; the gospel went out from their church all around Macedonia and Achaia, covering modern Greece and Macedonia, a very large area. Paul is very expressive in his description of this; he says that the gospel 'rang out' or literally, 'trumpeted' or 'thundered' from amongst them.[18]

It is an important aspect of leadership faith to trust the Holy Spirit to work in our new converts and our new churches. There are so many stories from our own era of missionaries having to pull out (for example, in parts of China as the communists took over), yet the church is still growing amazingly. In Thessalonica the church grew amazingly as the result of a good apostolic foundation having been laid which included New Testament truth, evident power of the Holy Spirit, teaching on suffering, and an expectation of mission.

Apostolic Ministry is Not Static

As there has been a growing recognition of the relevance of apostolic ministry today, particularly amongst new church networks, so there has also been an unfortunate development of a static or formalised understanding of this apostolic ministry. Even among new churches, there can be an almost institutional expectation that they will see apostolic ministry visiting their church every six months, or assisting at four elders' meetings a year. Yet one of the reasons for the letter to the Thessalonians is that the apostle could *not* come. Indeed, Paul quite often had to write about why he could not visit a particular church. There is a vibrant dynamic about the New Testament, such that even when there was no institutional provision of regular oversight visits, there was still remarkable growth and development. And the absence of apostolic visits occurred for a number of different reasons.

- **Satan hinders**

   In the case of the Thessalonians, Paul said that Satan hindered him from visiting them.[19] It is interesting that Paul could discern the difference between the Spirit of Jesus not allowing him to do something[20] and Satan hindering him; he was conscious of the warfare dimension of his apostolic mission. We need to be similarly conscious and sensitive both to the working of the Holy Spirit and the strategies of the devil. Prayer is important in this context, though it seems that even when we pray, Satan sometimes succeeds in hindering the advance of the gospel; yet the cause of the gospel did ultimately triumph, because of the effectiveness of this new church.

What do we do, then, when Satan seems to hinder our progress in mission? We need an effective alternative strategy. When Satan hindered, Paul did not bemoan his fate but thought of a creative solution; he sent Timothy on what was probably his first assignment as a young leader on Paul's team.[21] Satan may stop an effective apostle, but the result is that somebody else gets released into effective ministry!

It was not particularly convenient to send Timothy at that time. Paul was on his own in Athens and not enjoying it very much, and would not therefore have sent Timothy unless he had been really passionately concerned about the Thessalonians. Timothy was inexperienced, but Paul could describe him with confidence as 'our brother and God's fellow-worker'.[22] The result was that Timothy developed his leadership gifting, the Thessalonians were encouraged, and the whole church throughout the ages has the benefit of this letter which would not otherwise have been written!

Nevertheless, Paul was more than concerned about the efforts of the devil; he was even afraid, it says, because he knew the intensity of the devil's efforts to trip up new converts.[23] Paul afraid? Surely not! Isn't this negative confession? No, it is the reality of experience in mission. There is a balance to what I said earlier about trusting in the work of the grace of God; we are also to recognise the strength of what the devil might do, and therefore to be diligent in prayer and in laying a strong, biblical emphasis on discipleship.

- **Moving on**

  Another reason given in the New Testament for Paul not visiting churches was that he wanted to move on to the next mission field. Indeed, he was pleading with the church in Corinth to sort out their problems so that he could go on to regions beyond them.[24] There is an urgency about our mission which means that Christian apostolic leaders must not spend too much time in the maintenance and oversight of what already exists. It is not that Paul did not care about Corinth which was, after all, a relatively new church, but that his pressing urgency was to take the gospel into the regions beyond. Local churches in established situations must be willing to release leaders with an apostolic or evangelistic call to move on, even if they feel their church is not yet ready to do without them.

- **A question of priorities**

  Paul even seems to suggest that visiting established churches is a lower priority than pioneering mission into new areas! I wonder how we would react in our well-established churches if we received a letter like the one Paul wrote to Rome. He says that although he longed to come to them, he could not do so because he had a higher priority, which was to preach the gospel where Christ was not known.[25] I believe there is an urgent need for those with genuine apostolic calling to leave behind what has been established and entrust it to the grace of God, and lead a thrust of the gospel into the unreached areas of the world.

Relational Leadership Style

In writing to a church experiencing suffering, Paul reminded them that he had modelled a relevant leadership style. I believe that leadership style is one of the major issues facing the church in many parts of the world, in terms of both spreading kingdom values and opposing wrong cultural values. Leadership in the world is often institutional and depends on symbols of external authority, such as wealth, titles or other trappings of position. Jesus was very clear that our leadership style is not to be like that of the Gentiles or the heathen,[26] and even told his disciples that they were not to be called by official religious titles like 'Father' or 'Rabbi'.[27] I know that in some cultures and languages it is inappropriate to address somebody older or respected without some verbal form denoting such respect; I believe we can accept culturally appropriate ways of honouring, but must resist *religious titles* and hierarchy.

Paul makes much of his warm, relational style of leadership in his letter to this persecuted church, and says things we would hardly dare say: '. . . how holy, righteous and blameless we were among you who believed'![28] It seems that he was just carried away by his confidence in his servant heart towards the Thessalonian church. He describes the church as 'our glory and joy'.[29] His decision to send Timothy was not coolly calculated but 'when we could stand it no longer'.[30] We see here not a cold, dispassionate academic or a senior religious figure doing his duty, but a fiery, passionate, almost desperate, apostle.

A relational style of leadership is particularly important when a church is facing persecution. When Paul says, 'You *know* what we were like!'[31] he is actually answering criticisms about his own conduct: 'He runs away when it gets tough; he does not really care.' Receiving criticism, even from fellow Christians, is one of the perils of pioneer mission, and can have a bad effect on the fledgling church when the apostle is not there. I recall on one occasion hearing that a lady who had opposed my ministry in a church in Ukraine likened me to the Ukrainian equivalent of the 'village idiot' in comparison with the much more successful ministries around who had their own TV shows etc!

Examine Our Motives

1 Thessalonians, particularly chapter 2, contains Paul's answers to these accusations. He has examined his motives, which is a good thing for us to do from time to time when we are involved in mission, since it is possible to allow a passion for Christ and his gospel to become mixed up with personal ambition. Paul has examined himself and is confident that 'the appeal we make does not spring from error or impure motives, nor are we trying to trick you. On the contrary, we speak as men approved by God to be entrusted with the gospel. We are not trying to please men but God, who tests our hearts. You know we never used flattery, nor did we put on a mask to cover up greed'.[32]

The word 'error' denotes deceit, and challenges us to ask ourselves, is our ministry an open book? Is it clear who we are and that we are consistent with what we believe?

The Greek word used here for 'impure' usually referred to sexual immorality, and indeed, there were many travelling teachers at the time that Paul was writing, whose morals did not bear close scrutiny. Commentaries differ as to whether 'impure' in this context is specific to sexual immorality, or is more general in meaning. I think that in the context of Christian leadership in the twenty-first century, we are safer to assume it is specific. Too often, I read in the Christian press of leadership breaking down because of sexual immorality. Sometimes such behaviour hardly even seems to be disciplined, though immorality amongst leaders can cripple our mission.

Paul did not use trickery or flattery, words which imply manipulation in the context of preaching. The power and passion of preaching are such that they can be misused; we can (but must not) employ powerful and persuasive oratory to recruit people to our own selfish ends. Paul was not a people-pleaser. He was willing to become 'all things to all men' (1 Cor. 9:22) in order to gain some with the gospel, but he did not water down his message under the guise of cultural adaptation, in order to please his hearers.

Paul did not 'put on a mask to cover up greed'. The misuse of money is a massive hindrance to mission. It is beyond the scope of this book to go into this in detail, but the dangers include westerners living at an inappropriate level of luxury in third world contexts, and indigenous leaders in church planting situations becoming dependent on western funds, which can cause them to be out of touch with their own people. It is important that even in situations of poverty, churches are taught to support their own pastors. Alternatively, culturally and economically appropriate small businesses may be set up to provide for both pastor and community and thus avoid becoming dependent on western funding.

As I have said, we need to keep testing our motives as leaders. I am aware of certain landmarks in my own history. I was originally a very ambitious person, particularly when I was in secular work, and I remember the time when that had to die. When I left banking, the Chief Executive of the international bank for which I worked told me that he could understand me giving up the money, but not the opportunity of career development. He pointed out that in the sort of church I would be serving, I could not even become a bishop! He had obviously discerned something about me! There was a danger for me that even, when I had left secular work, I might become ambitious for a wider or international ministry. I remember the moment when, kneeling in my study and banging my fist on the floor, I said to God that if he wanted me only to serve a small company of people on an estate in north-east Bedford, that was fine by me. That dealt with my career ambitions! When Scilla and I first started serving the church full-time, I had no salary and we had to live by faith, which dealt for that time (!) with any ambition for money! Let us be careful never to see ministry as a hierarchy, with opportunities for promotion up the company ladder! This attitude could so easily sneak in without our realising it.

Sharing Our Lives

Paul set an example here of hard work and of not being a burden to the church.[33] We have already seen how he described himself as being like a nursing mother amongst them, and said that he not only shared the gospel but created a family atmosphere in the church by sharing his life. We, too, must share our lives with people, and not just be on a platform or in a missionary compound. A young pastor came up to me and Scilla after I had ministered at a conference in a poorer part of the world. With tears in his eyes, he told us that this was the first time he had attended a conference at which western guest speakers had shared the same accommodation and meals as those to whom they were ministering, instead of being put up in a separate hotel, being driven to the meetings and eating their meals separately. I was grieved that western conference speakers should give such an impression of being separate from those to whom they minister.

I was recently in another country, where the temperature was in the mid-forties. I was preaching that evening, and the indigenous team of church leaders I was travelling with had booked an air-conditioned hotel room for me to rest in before the meeting and arranged for dinner to be brought to the room. I asked what they were doing and where they were eating, and they said they would wait outside. I protested that this was not right, so we ordered eight meals from room service and arranged for the eight of us to sleep on the three beds and across the floor of the room I had been allocated!

Paul said to the Corinthian Christians that he was like a father amongst them,[34] responsible for their teaching and nurturing. He saw the need to urge them forward, but with encouragement. He complimented them, reminded them what God had done amongst them, and commended their zeal. This is what fathers do when they are encouraging their children. It is the appropriate leadership style as we minister to suffering people.

This epistle, which we have considered in some detail, is written by an apostle who is passionate for world mission to a missionary-oriented church. This ought to be the situation today. I believe God wants to raise up many with apostolic, evangelistic and 'helps' ministries, passionate for world mission, to join together to plant churches, reach new nations with the gospel, go where the gospel has not been preached and reach out to the poor and the destitute. I believe God wants to create churches which identify with this mission and send people to join it. They need to be churches which give themselves and their finances to this mission. And in order to inspire and motivate such mission, I believe leadership in God's church today needs to be as passionate for the lost, as flexible and as relational as Paul evidently was in relation to the church in Thessalonica.

Notes

1 John Piper, *Let the Nations be Glad*, p. 74
2 2 Corinthians 1:8–11; 6:4–10; 11:23–29; 12:7–10
3 2 Corinthians 11:28
4 1 Thessalonians 3:6–10
5 See 1 Thessalonians 2:6–8
6 Acts 17:1–10
7 1 Thessalonians 3:5
8 Acts 9:31
9 John Piper, *Let the Nations be Glad*, p. 92
10 John 16:33
11 1 Peter 5:9
12 James 1:2
13 Acts 14:22
14 Dietrich Bonhoeffer, *The Court of Discipleship* (Macmillan, 1963), p. 99
15 Matthew 13:21
16 A misunderstanding of Acts 17:2
17 1 Thessalonians 1:9
18 1 Thessalonians 1:7,8
19 1 Thessalonians 2:18
20 Acts 16:7
21 1 Thessalonians 3:2
22 1 Thessalonians 3:2
23 1 Thessalonians 3:5
24 2 Corinthians 10:15,16
25 Romans 15:20–22
26 Matthew 20:25–28
27 Matthew 23:8–12
28 1 Thessalonians 2:10
29 1 Thessalonians 2:20
30 1 Thessalonians 3:1,2
31 See 1 Thessalonians 1:5
32 1 Thessalonians 2:3–5
33 2 Corinthians 11:9; 12:16
34 1 Corinthians 4:15

Chapter Twelve

Who Will Go?[1]

In the nineteenth century, friends of Dr David Livingstone, the famous missionary and explorer, wrote him the following message while he was away in Africa: 'We would like to send other men to you. Have you found a good road into your area yet?' Livingstone replied, 'If you have men who will only come if you have a good road, I don't want them. I want men who will come if there is no road at all.'[2]

The family of churches for which I am part of the leadership team had a prophetic word right at the time of the formation of our movement, to the effect that 'There are no well-worn paths ahead of you'. God was saying to us that he wanted the characteristic of our network of churches to be pioneering, seeking to carve out new paths in the fulfilment of his purposes.

Today, in many parts of the world, people are still waiting to hear the good news of Jesus Christ for the very first time. There are obviously many more literal roads than in David Livingstone's time, though for some people groups to hear the gospel there will still need to be a literal road cut where no path currently exists!

However, for many people, serving God's purposes will involve them in crossing borders of a different kind. For some it will be linguistic, social or cultural borders, while for others it will be the opening up of new areas by the application of scientific and technological discoveries that will speed up and extend the advance of the gospel worldwide.

Responding to the Challenge of Our Generation

Each new generation faces a new set of challenges but also has open to them an abundance of new opportunities. Hebrews 11 demonstrates how each new generation had to exercise faith in God in a way for which there had been no precedent in previous generations. Abel had to offer a sacrifice from his flocks; Enoch simply walked with God and then disappeared; Noah had to build a boat, where faith had not required the building of boats before![3] As we go on through that wonderful chapter describing the pioneers of faith, we realise that each one had to respond to God's word for their own time. For some, that meant enduring persecution and even martyrdom,[4] but even that was accomplished by faith. At the start of the twenty-first century we are presented with many challenges and opportunities for new ventures of faith, as we and the local churches of which we are part seek to become involved in God's great plan to bless the nations.

Poverty Gap

There is, for example, a growing disparity between rich and poor. Jimmy Carter, the former US President, called this the twenty-first century's ultimate challenge, and went on to remark that there is an insensitivity or unawareness in the rich, developed world, of the plight of people in the poor under-developed world, and that the chasm is growing; Carter said that he didn't see any encouraging movements to address it either in the US, Europe, Japan or in other rich countries.[5] I believe that there is already a growing movement in the evangelical church challenging this unawareness. However, it needs to grow much more if it is to appear on the radar screens of world statesmen and significantly affect the world in which we live.

There have obviously always been both rich and poor within every society, and much of Scripture addresses this issue. One major difference today is that the gap between rich and poor is now also a gap between different nations and economic systems, so that those travelling from one context to another have to make serious adjustments in their lifestyles and expectations. David Burnett, writing in 1996, comments that, 'When William Carey left for India in 1797, on average the standard of living in Britain was on a par with that of India. By 1900 the standard of living in Britain was at least 4 times that of India, while today it is more like 40 times'.[6] Because the people sent into a nation with the gospel are often from a more affluent nation, this very issue complicates the gospel and people's response to it. Along with the genuine receiving of the gospel, some situations arise of an unhealthy dependency on the west, in which the benefits of employment or other financial advantage compete with the gospel as a motivation for joining a church planted from overseas.

Furthermore, the habit of using overseas funds to pay pastors in the medium or long-term can complicate the relationships between indigenous pastors and their own people; pastors can become alienated from their flock and even in some situations become the only ones with a steady income. Muslims often (and usually falsely) accuse new believers of having been 'purchased'. This certainly complicates our message in a way probably not experienced to such an extent before, in the whole history of missions. It can even be a factor in nations which are a mixture of first and third world, such as South Africa, where white South Africans from prosperous suburbs move into poorer areas to take the gospel, but have a very different lifestyle expectation from those they go to.

Today, the rich nations of the world have 20 per cent of the world's population, yet control 71 per cent of global trade in goods and services and 58 per cent of foreign direct investment, and have 91 per cent of all internet users. The so-called 'North' – Europe, America and Japan – receives annually in debt repayments from poorer countries between $20 billion and $40 billion more than is given out in aid. Even such 'aid' is often a misnomer as it is more usually a commercial loan, often with political or economic strings attached, such as a requirement to purchase goods or services from the 'donor' country.

Job Creation

As we have seen, the Bible witnesses to a God who works on behalf of the weak, the vulnerable and the poor, and is concerned about issues of justice. This must include global economic justice. However, we recognise that another of the major obstacles to such justice is corruption, mismanagement and bureaucracy within many of the poor countries with even some dictators treating national treasures as their personal saving accounts.

God's people therefore must help meet the needs of some of the poorest peoples of the world, not only by direct giving but by encouraging and participating in long-term investment for the benefit of the poor, such as job creation schemes and low interest credit to sustain small-scale enterprises run by the poor. However, finance alone is not sufficient. If a workforce is to take full advantage of the economic opportunities laid before them, attention must also be given to their education and health. Programmes to educate, develop indigenous skills and provide greater access to new technologies must become priorities alongside the delivery of better healthcare.

Globalisation, though in some ways a threat to the developing world, also opens a wide door for the active involvement of Christian business personnel, economists, lawyers, politicians, health workers, educationalists and many others. It is as we act as salt and light in the world, both individually and corporately, that the church will fulfil its mandate to be not only a witness to the kingdom of God but the agent of the kingdom's advance.

Mega Cities

Another feature of life in the twenty-first century is the growing urbanisation of the planet. Vast numbers of people are still moving from the countryside into towns and cities. In 1950 it was estimated that around 30 per cent of the world was urbanised, but by 1990 this figure had risen to 51 per cent. During this same forty-year period, urbanisation in the less economically developed nations of the world doubled from 17 per cent to 34 per cent, particularly in Africa, Asia and South America.

In the world today there are well over three hundred cities with a population of over one million. Some have even reached the status of mega-cities with populations in excess of ten million, for example, Tokyo, Mexico City, Sao Paulo, New York and Mumbai.

The economic and social problems that arise from urbanisation are well known. Pictures of the 'shanty towns' that spring up in or around large cities in the developing world often hit our TV screens, as do documentaries on the 'problems of the inner city'. Over-crowding, pollution, lack of housing and employment, crime, drugs, prostitution, vandalism, truancy, family and community breakdown all combine to make urban living in today's world a tough option. There is a massive challenge for churches to find new ways into the mega-cities of the world in order to reach the varied communities within them.

Migration

I have already referred to the recent phenomenon of large-scale migrations of refugees and asylum seekers: people trying to further their education, or to escape poverty, conflict, war and other political difficulties, including the ugly resurgence of 'ethnic cleansing'. The United Nations High Commissioner for Refugees (UNHCR) particularly deals with asylum seekers, refugees returning home and displaced people within their own country, and the scale of the problem can be gauged by the fact that at the end of January 2003, the UNHCR alone had some twenty million people on their books! Here, once again, is an opportunity for the church to become involved as an agent of reconciliation and change within its local community, and with practical demonstrations of love and caring that build important bridges into communities so that the gospel can be shared across cultures.

Suffering Children

Another new road needs to be made into the lives of children right across the world. At the present time, it is estimated that some twenty million children are involved in child labour, many in the most appalling conditions. In 1996 the UN reported that some 142 million children lived on the world's streets, while other reports estimate that something like ten to twelve million children are involved in the sex trade.

Over the last ten years, many children have been forced to become child soldiers, and the ravages of war have seen some twelve million children left homeless, ten million psychologically traumatised and a further five million physically disabled in nations such as Sierra Leone, Rwanda and Northern Uganda.

Children also suffer alongside their parents as a result of famine and natural disasters but are often more vulnerable to sickness and disease. In many countries, children are infected with the HIV virus and have witnessed the death of parents and relatives. It is still a scandal that on average, more than thirty thousand children under the age of five die each day from malnutrition and easily preventable diseases. Hiroshi Nakajina, the Director General of the World Health Organisation, calls this 'the silent genocide on our planet'.[7]

As we consider our mission, we need to wake up to the fact that not only is 60 per cent of the world's population under twenty-five years of age, but also that 30 per cent is actually under fifteen years of age. It should be noted further that 85 per cent of those under fifteen years of age live in the developing world and are therefore often subject to many of the hardships and traumas we have just outlined.

In today's world, some 1.1 billion people lack access to clean water, while a further 2.4 billion lack adequate sanitation. Add to this the increase in natural disasters and it is not too difficult to understand the statement from World Vision that 'every 3 seconds a child dies as a direct result of poverty'.

Poverty, of course, comes in different guises. For some in the world it consists simply of a lack of essentials like food, clean water, adequate housing, healthcare, employment, schools and good roads. For others its focus is a lack of education, knowledge, skills or access to new technologies. For still others, it is the inability to have any meaningful influence over their current well-being or future life.

Languages

Another road that needs to be built is a linguistic one. We are faced with the need for communication in many languages. Wycliffe Bible Translators have clear evidence that once a people group have the Scriptures in their own 'heart' language, the spread of the gospel accelerates among them. The issue of 'heart language' or 'mother tongue' is so important. At one 'Asian outreach' meeting in our church, we worshipped in English, Punjabi and Tamil with contributions from different worship teams, and I then consulted the other leaders present as to which language I should be translated into as I preached. The Tamil pastor suggested that as all the Tamils present understood English, I should be translated into Punjabi. When I gave an appeal at the end, English and Punjabi speakers came forward for prayer, but no Tamil speakers! At that point, the Tamil pastor jumped up and began to speak in Tamil, summarising my message and giving another invitation, to which several Tamils responded. I said to him afterwards, 'I thought you said they all understood English!' 'Oh, they understand English all right,' he replied, 'but it doesn't speak to their hearts!' So with the Scriptures, people are able to understand and respond much more readily when they receive God's word in their own 'heart' language.

The Scriptures are vital to the effective discipling of people, teaching, worship and leadership training. This is why Wycliffe currently has some one thousand five hundred translations in progress, many into languages which have never been written down before. New technology, such as computers and satellite phones, is speeding up the translation process and Wycliffe has a vision that by 2025, in partnership with others, they will have begun a translation project for every people group in the world that needs one (approximately three thousand). Our churches need to catch that vision and get involved.

The Need is Not the Cause

I have spent most of this chapter, so far, outlining the major needs of the poorer peoples of the world. However, despite this appalling litany of needs, in the end all the need does is arouse our compassion, lead us to pray and turn us to God. The need does not in itself constitute the call. The call arises from God's promises and his clearly-declared intention that his people should be a community on the move with the gospel, extending his kingdom across the world. Immediately after the curse upon the nations at Babel in Genesis 11, in the very next chapter, in fact, comes the promise to Abraham: '. . . all peoples on earth will be blessed through you'.[8]

The psalms are full of promises of the glory of God filling the earth: 'Declare his glory among the nations, his marvellous deeds among all peoples';[9] 'Ascribe to the LORD, O families of nations, ascribe to the LORD glory and strength . . . Say among the nations, "The LORD reigns." '[10] And the Father promises his Son, the Messiah: 'Ask of me, and I will make the nations your inheritance, the ends of the earth your possession'.[11]

We also have the privilege of knowing the end of the story. The book of Revelation encourages our faith and motivates our mission when it describes the scene in heaven, as those from every ethnic group worship God together: '. . . there before me was a great multitude that no-one could count, from every nation, tribe, people and language, standing before the throne and in front of the Lamb'.[12] As I said at the end of Chapter Two, this is the ultimate goal of our mission.

Obedient Faith

Like Abraham and every other man and woman of faith throughout history, we are to exercise faith and obedience at the point in history where we find ourselves. Abraham had to exercise faith and obedience at the time he was living, in order for the promise to be fulfilled. Indeed, even when he had received the first fulfilment of the promise in the birth of a son to Sarah, he was challenged to exercise that faith even more when he was told to take his son Isaac and offer him as a sacrifice. He did so in obedience, believing that God could even raise Isaac from the dead.[13] I believe it is significant that on this occasion, Abraham's obedient faith was followed by God making an oath, declaring that the promise and its fulfilment were now absolutely certain. God said, 'I swear by myself, declares the LORD, that *because you have done this* and have not withheld your son, your only son, I will surely bless you and make your descendants as numerous as the stars in the sky and the sand on the seashore. Your descendants will take possession of the cities of their enemies, and through your offspring all nations on earth will be blessed, *because you have obeyed me*',[14] (my emphasis). It seems that in some way, Abraham's faith and obedience contributed, and indeed, became the reason for the assurance that the promise of the blessing of the nations would be fulfilled. I believe that when we take similar steps as individuals and churches, our obedience, along with the obedience of past generations of missionaries, will constitute the basis for God's declaration that his promise will be fulfilled.

God Speaks to a Young Man

Another scripture records the experience of a young man facing a crucial time in his nation's history, just as we now face crucial times in the world's history and in the unfolding of God's purposes on earth. A king who had reigned for more than fifty years and brought stability to the nation had just died. What did the future hold? Larger nations were growing in power and threatening the very existence of the nation of Israel. The king who had died was Uzziah, and the young man was Isaiah, probably in his late teens; he went into the temple and saw an awesome vision of the glory of God. This vision was to characterise the whole of his future ministry. Isaiah has become known in different ways as the gospel prophet, the missionary prophet, and the prophet who not only spoke out against the ill-treatment of the poor but promised blessing to the poor.

Of his experience, Isaiah wrote, 'I saw the Lord' (see Is. 6:1). Many of us base our serving of God on what he has done for us; that is wonderful, and comes later in Isaiah's vision experience. But first, Isaiah saw the Lord in all his glory. God is high and exalted – too high to be questioned, only to be submitted to. He is so awesome, so powerful and so glorious that I am privileged even to be in his presence; the further privilege of being allowed to serve him is a bonus. He is surrounded by flaming, burning, worshipping beings, by cherubim and seraphim around his throne. He is unutterably holy, totally separate from his creation. He does not have to give an account to anybody. We live in an age that so exalts humanity, that it can appear to us as if God has to justify himself and his actions to our puny little minds. If we give in to the spirit of the age in this matter, we will live in constant insecurity about God himself.

God-Centred Mission

This overwhelming sense of the glory and the greatness of God became the principle characteristic of all Isaiah's writings. His prophecies are all God-centred, even when he is addressing practical, down-to-earth human issues. When he encounters the perceived power of humanity, as displayed in the nations around Israel, he looks at it in comparison with God, and concludes, 'All men are like grass, and all their glory is like the flowers of the field. The grass withers and the flowers fall, because the breath of the LORD blows on them . . . The grass withers and the flowers fall, but the word of our God stands for ever'.[15] Empires seem impregnable, then God blows on them, and they can disappear almost overnight! It is not many years ago that Christians, along with most westerners, saw communism as impregnable. We prayed for our persecuted brothers and sisters, and daring evangelistic pioneers went through the Iron Curtain, smuggling Bibles. Then one day God blew, the grass withered and the flower of communism fell.

When I was at school, I can just remember most countries in the atlas being pink, representing where the British Empire held sway (we used old atlases in our school!). Then God blew – even the Prime Minister at the time described it as a 'wind of change'! – and the British Empire waned rapidly as one country after another gained its independence. The same chapter of Isaiah goes on to contrast the glory of God with human counsel: no one gives him advice; the nations of the earth are no more to him than a drop in the bucket or dust on the scales; even the greatest men are no bigger than grasshoppers by comparison with him.[16]

Isaiah also contrasts the greatness of God with our human weariness and disappointment as we wait to see the accomplishment of all we have dreamed about. God says, 'Do you not know? Have you not heard? The LORD is the everlasting God, the Creator of the ends of the earth. He will not grow tired or weary, and his understanding no-one can fathom.'[17] When he scorns the nothingness, the uselessness and the pointlessness of human idols, Isaiah still focuses on the greatness of God himself, 'I am the first and I am the last; apart from me there is no God. Who then is like me? Let him proclaim it.'[18]

Isaiah's vision of the greatness of God made him a life-long worshipper. In our day, too, we are privileged to see the restoration of wonderful worship to the church of Jesus Christ. Whenever God moves in his church there is a restoration of worship. It is important that in our concentration on mission and on the great task before us, we do not fail to be centred on God in worship. There is even a danger, in some modern songs, of worship itself becoming human-centred so that we concentrate on *how we feel*, rather than *who God is*. Let us declare the wonders of God; let us declare them to the nations! Let us declare the glories of God! Let the functioning of spiritual gifts in our churches be such that people can say, 'God is among you!' If, in John Piper's words, which I quoted in Chapter Two, worship is the object of mission, then those concerned with mission must first be worshippers.

A Vision of God's Dwelling Place

However, Isaiah's vision was not only of God, but also of his dwelling place. He says that the train of his robe filled the temple. For Isaiah, the picture of the temple, the city and the mountain, where God dwells with people, became a major theme of his prophetic message.

- In the city, God's presence is to be made known to the whole world. All the nations will come to worship there, and it will be 'the joy of the whole earth';[19] it will grow, spreading out to the right and to the left.[20]

- The mountain of God, again speaking of his dwelling place, will be raised above the other mountains.[21]
- As we have seen, one of God's purposes in the earth is to have a place to dwell; indeed, in the book of Revelation the final summary of everything is that God is dwelling with people.[22] And it is now God's church that is being built to be the place where God dwells. 'In him the whole building is joined together and rises to become a holy temple in the Lord. And in him you too are being built together to become a dwelling in which God lives by his Spirit.'[23]

So Isaiah's vision was also of the glorious dwelling place of God, intended in our day to be the end-time glorious church.

A Vision for the Whole World

Isaiah's vision also related to the whole world; not only did God's glory fill the temple, but the whole earth was full of his glory. This became another significant theme in Isaiah's writings. He became the prophet who foretold the gathering in of all the nations, and what Isaiah saw as a prophetic vision will one day become true in reality. 'For the earth will be filled with the knowledge of the glory of the LORD, as the waters cover the sea.' . . . 'In that day the Root of Jesse will stand as a banner for the peoples; the nations will rally to him, and his place of rest will be glorious.'[24] This prophecy even specifically incorporates Arab peoples, or what is now the Muslim world, into this blessing. 'In that day there will be a highway from Egypt to Assyria . . . The Egyptians and Assyrians will worship together. In that day Israel will be the third, along with Egypt and Assyria, a blessing on the earth'.[25] Here we see the two superpowers of Isaiah's time uniting with Israel and accepting each other, because each is accepted by God. Alec Motyer describes it as 'a case in point of the Lord's purpose to unite the world in his worship.'[26]

Grace to Fulfil Our Mission

God's unmerited grace became the basis for the fulfilment of Isaiah's glorious vision. First, Isaiah realised that he himself could not do anything to fulfil it. He recognised his own uselessness: he was undone; he could not speak; he was lost in sin; his own lips were unclean and so were those of all the people. The altar, which corresponds to the cross today, deals with that issue. At the cross we are forgiven and released from failure and the power of the sin that holds us. It is important to notice that in Isaiah's case, as for us, this was done on the basis of grace alone. Isaiah made no contribution, except to cry out his need. This shows us clearly that it is God who takes the initiative in salvation, and in sending us to the ends of the earth. Without God's gracious initiative, Isaiah could do nothing to fulfil the glorious visions he was seeing. His only contributions were his repentance which, in itself, as we know is graciously granted by God, and his realisation of his total inadequacy.

What is Heaven Saying Today?

Finally, Isaiah's vision became the means of his commission. What we see becomes the basis of how we are sent to do it. Isaiah heard the voice of heaven. What was heaven saying then? The same as heaven is saying today: 'Whom shall I send? And who will go for us?' (Is. 6:8). The fulfilment of the glorious vision of Isaiah depends on people being sent, and following Isaiah's release from the power of all that would hold him back, came his declaration of his availability. 'Here am I, send me!' (v. 8).

Isaiah heard the voice of heaven. He responded to the voice of heaven. Heaven is still calling. I believe 'Who will go?' is still the cry from the heart of heaven as God looks down and sees our needy world. 'Who will go?' Will our churches be missional churches? Will we be a missionary people? Will we respond as Isaiah did? This is what the church is on earth for so now let us fulfil our glorious commission and go to plant churches and extend the reign of God in this world until Jesus returns to bring the kingdom of God in all its fullness, to usher in a new heaven and new earth in which righteousness/justice dwells. Maranatha. Come Lord Jesus!

Notes

1 I am indebted to my good friend Mike Frisby of City Church Cambridge for the statistical research in this chapter.
2 http://www.sermons.org/commitment.html
3 Hebrews 11:1–38
4 Hebrews 11:37
5 Newsweek, 24 May 1999, p. 25
6 David Burnett, *The Healing of the Nations* (Paternoster, 1996), p. 17
7 Quoted in Noam Chomsky, *Powers and Prospects: Reflections on Human Nature and the Social Order* (Pluto, 1996), p. 106
8 Genesis 12:3
9 Psalm 96:3
10 Psalm 96:7,10
11 Psalm 2:8
12 Revelation 7:9
13 Hebrews 11:19
14 Genesis 22:16–18
15 Isaiah 40:6–8
16 Isaiah 40:15–17
17 Isaiah 40:28
18 Isaiah 44:6,7
19 Psalm 48:2
20 Isaiah 54:3

21 Isaiah 2:2
22 Revelation 21:3
23 Ephesians 2:21,22
24 Habakkuk 2:14; Isaiah 11:10
25 Isaiah 19:23,24
26 Alec Motyer, *The Prophecy of Isaiah*, p. 169

DEMOLISHING STRONGHOLDS
Effective Strategies for Spiritual Warfare

David Devenish

David Devenish shares insight drawn from many years of personal experience in helping people break free from strongholds that have bound them. In this no-nonsense guide to spiritual warfare, he gives us effective strategies for spiritual warfare which include:

- Having a biblical model for understanding the enemy's strategies and dealing with them
- Keeping a balance between the reality of Satan and the demonic realm, our responsibility for our actions, and the absolute sovereignty of God
- Understanding that strongholds are wrong thinking and learning to use godly power to pull them down.
- Understanding our authority in Christ
- Knowing our weapons and using them

'David's book on demolishing spiritual strongholds is the clearest biblical teaching on the subject I have ever read. This book should be mandatory reading for all serious Christians.'
Barney Coombs, International Director,
Salt & Light Ministries

'I was captivated and intrigued by the timely warning in Demolishing Strongholds. *David Devenish has provided valuable insights on spiritual warfare. This book should be required reading for all who seek to advance the Kingdom of God through intercession.'*
John Paul Jackson, Founder and President,
Streams Ministries International

THE FATHER YOU'VE BEEN WAITING FOR
Portrait of a Perfect Dad

Mark Stibbe

It has been said that today's generation of young people – those in the 14–35 age bracket – are the generation of divorced parents, absent fathers and broken homes. More than any other in history, this generation is the 'fatherless generation'. Everywhere people are asking, 'where is the love?'

In this book, popular author and speaker Mark Stibbe answers that question by pointing to a story told 2,000 years ago by Jesus of Nazareth. The story tells of a father who demonstrates the qualities of a perfect dad. More than that, the story paints the clearest picutre of what Jesus thought God is really like.

This book is a source of extraordinary hope for people of all ages and all beliefs (and indeed no beliefs). In provides a wonderfully accessible introduction to 'The Father You've Been Waiting For'. It also contains many new insights into a story loved by millions and known as 'the parable of parables'.

'If you are seraching for answers, if you are yearning for wholeness, if you are interested in exploring the meaning of life and/or the relevance of the God of the Bible in the twenty-first century, then Mark's book is definitely worth a read. In fact, this is a must-read for anyone who wants a direct, honest explanation of how the remarkable God who created the universe, loves and is interested in an exclusive, intimate, life-transforming relationship with you. Who knows, it may well contribute to changing your life – forever!'

Diane Louise Jordan

THE GOSPEL-DRIVEN CHURCH
Retrieving Classical Ministries for
Contemporary Revivalism

Ian Stackhouse

Charismatic renewal has at the core of its ideology an inspiration for revival. This is a laudable aspiration, but in recent years, in the absence of large-scale evangelistic impact, such a vision has encouraged a faddist mentality among church leaders in this part of the body of Christ.

The Gospel-Driven Church documents this development and the numerous theological and pastoral distortions that take place when genuine revival fervour transmutes into revivalism. Moreover, Ian Stackhouse aims to show how a retrieval of some of the core practices of the church, such as preaching, sacraments, the laying on of hands and prayer are essential at this crucial stage in the trajectory of the renewal movement. He commends to church leaders a recovery of these means of grace as a way of keeping the church centred on the gospel rather than mere pragmatic concerns about size and numbers.

'A model of careful biblical and spiritual discernment, both appreciative and cautionary. I find Ian a most welcome ally in our "stay against confusion".'
Eugene Peterson, Professor Emeritus of Spiritual Theology, Regent College, Vancouver, Canada

'Combines the scholarly, the prophetic and the burningly relevant, in strong and equal measures.'
Greg Haslam, Senior Minister, Westminster Chapel, London